THE TESTS OF FAITH

THE TESTS OF FAITH

J. A. MOTYER

INTER-VARSITY PRESS

INTER-VARSITY PRESS

Inter-Varsity Fellowship
39 Bedford Square, London WC1B 3EY

Inter-Varsity Christian Fellowship
Box F, Downers Grove, Illinois 60515

© INTER-VARSITY PRESS, LONDON
First Edition August 1970
Reprinted January 1972

ISBN 0 85110 349 9

The Bible text used in this book is from the
Revised Standard Version of the Bible, copyrighted
1946 and 1952.

Printed in Great Britain by
Hunt Barnard Printing Ltd,
Aylesbury, Bucks

CONTENTS

'In this you rejoice, though now for a little while you may have to suffer various trials, so that the genuineness of your faith, more precious than gold which though perishable is tested by fire, may redound to praise and glory and honour at the revelation of Jesus Christ' (1 Peter 1: 6, 7).

PREFACE

The studies which this book contains have had a considerable pre-history, and I am grateful to the present publishers
for giving them this new extension of life.

The material first began to be collected for the mid-week
Bible study at St Luke's Church, Hampstead, London, where
I had the privilege of being Vicar. Indeed, I would dedicate
this book to my friends, the members of St Luke's, were it not
that dedications are now somewhat out of fashion, and (more
important) that this volume is altogether too mean and un-
worthy a token of appreciation of the joys and benefits to me
of my five years in that happy place.

In September 1968 I took the Letter of James as the subject for the Bible Readings at the Christian Holiday Crusade,
organized by the Movement for World Evangelization
at Filey, and the New Mildmay Press published a limited
edition of what was then said.

For the purposes of this present book, the studies have been
almost entirely re-written, considerably expanded, and fur-
nished with an Introduction and footnotes, for when the
Inter-Varsity Press expressed interest in re-issuing the earlier
book, it seemed to me a pity not to take the opportunity of
introducing in the text and notes matter which limitations of
time had necessarily excluded from the Bible Readings as
spoken and printed, and also of tidying out of sight those sty-
listic features which are appropriate to the pulpit but angular
in print.

7

In all these matters I have been greatly helped on my way by Miss Clare Richards of the Inter-Varsity Press, and am glad to have the opportunity of expressing my appreciation of her help.

Studies such as these are not and cannot be exhaustive treatments of the text. A main line of analysis and comment is offered, but where there is room for legitimate difference of opinion I have, on the whole, done no more than state and try to justify the interpretation which seems to me most satisfactory. No word is infallible except that of Scripture as originally given. May each reader, then, by God's goodness, find in this book something to help in understanding what the Spirit of God caused to be written for our learning. But, as is our God-given privilege, under the authority of Scripture, let each be persuaded in his own mind.

Tyndale Hall,   J. A. MOTYER
Bristol, 8.

INTRODUCTION

Very often we can expect light to be thrown on the meaning of a Bible book or passage if we can discover some facts about the author, the time of origin and the circumstances of the people to whom it was first addressed. In the case of the Letter of James, however, this approach is almost wholly denied to us. Authorship, date and destination are all matters of some uncertainty.[1]

Authorship

There are three men called James in the New Testament: James the son of Zebedee (Mk. 1:19; Acts 12:2, *etc.*), James the son of Alphaeus (Mk. 3:18), usually identified with James the younger (Mk. 15:40), and James the Lord's brother (Mt. 13:55; Acts 12:17; 15:13ff.; 1 Cor. 15:7; Gal. 1:19; 2:9). It is generally urged that James the son of Zebedee, martyred in AD 44, was too early removed from the Christian scene to be the author. It is obviously hard to argue either for or against the candidature of James the son of Alphaeus, since nothing more is known of him, though this does not necessarily rule him out. It would put him in the same category as Jude, known only for his name and his letter.

[1] For fuller treatment of these questions, see R. V. G. Tasker, *The General Epistle of James* (London, 1956); D. Guthrie (*New Testament Introduction*[2], London, 1970), pp. 736ff.; *The New Bible Dictionary* (London, 1962), *s.v.* James, Epistle of; C. L. Mitton, *The Epistle of James* (London, 1966); *The New Bible Commentary: Revised* (London, 1970).

Traditionally, however, authorship has been ascribed to James the Lord's brother, and he still appears the strongest candidate, though the arguments are by no means conclusive. The most direct link with this James appears in verbal resemblances between the letter and James' speech to the Council of Jerusalem, recorded in Acts 15:13–21.[2] As to the rest, it may be said that the obvious saturation of the letter with Old Testament atmosphere and illustrations well suits the portraiture of James in Acts.

Certainly, it is hardly likely that the letter is the work of a pseudonymous writer posing as either James the apostle or James the Lord's brother, for if this were the case it is extremely unlikely that he would have left his assumed identity so open to question. Furthermore, at the time when the letter of James was accepted in the early church as authoritative and part of the New Testament it was on the basis of a strict requirement of apostolic authority.

Date

James the Lord's brother was martyred in AD 62 (according to Josephus, *Antiquities* xx.9.1), but how early before this date he might have written his letter is impossible to say. The contents lack any positive pointer. Some hold that it was written before AD 50, but the evidence available is inconclusive and Guthrie simply says that the earlier rather than the later of these two dates is probably better.

Destination

The destination of the letter is given in the opening verse.

---

[2]These resemblances are all more apparent in Greek than in our English translations, but at best are a meagre evidence of authorship. *Cf.* Jas. 1:27 and Acts 15:14; Jas. 5:19,20 and Acts 15:19; Jas. 1:16,19; 2:5 and Acts 15:13,25.

Led on by the apparent meaning of this and by the continuing Old Testament content of the letter, some have preferred to think of it as addressed to scattered communities of Hebrew–Christians, but the more attractive interpretation sees in this verse an address to the Christian church in the world, described symbolically and correctly as God's 'twelve tribes'. This view will be more thoroughly examined and presented in the first of the following studies, but it may be observed here that such a description of the church would come naturally to a mind so impregnated by the truths and categories of Scripture as James'.

We are in the unfortunate position of having inherited 'Old Testament' as the title of the first and larger portion of the Bible. We need constantly to recall that such a description would have been meaningless to the Lord, His apostles and their contemporaries like James. They would have spoken of 'Moses and the prophets' (Lk. 24:27), 'Moses and the prophets and the psalms' (Lk. 24:44), 'the scriptures' (Lk. 24:27), 'the sacred writings' (2 Tim. 3:15), and so forth, and to them the Christian church was the current form and constitution of that people which God was gathering for Himself from among men. It is in this spirit that Paul sees Christians as the genuine 'descendants' of Abraham (Rom. 4:9–25) and 'Abraham's offspring, heirs according to promise' (Gal. 3:29). Thus also he says that 'we are the circumcision' (Phil. 3:3),[3] and indeed 'the Israel of God' (Gal. 6:16). It is notable that he does not say 'the new Israel', a description which occurs nowhere in the New Testament, but 'the Israel of God'. The 'new Israel' implies that somewhere an 'old' Israel

[3]RSV inserts the word 'true', but while this is not wholly misleading, it does not express the rigour of Paul's thought. He is not so much concerned with the contrast of 'true' with 'false' as with the contrast of 'real' with 'unreal'. It is as if he said, 'The circumcision practised by the Jews, and by their fellow-travellers who desire to impose this rite on you, has nothing whatever to do with God's ancient ordinance. We, we Christians, are the circumcision, the marked people of God.'

is to be found. This is not so. There is only one Israel, and that is the Christian church, the heirs of the promise and the people of God.

This line of truth goes hand in glove with the Letter of James. Without any incongruity, he takes figures like Abraham from the remote past and makes them express truths and principles for the Christian, for though people change, places alter and time passes the same people of God continues and the same immutable God is their Father. How reasonable then that James address the church spread throughout an unbelieving and alien world as 'the twelve tribes in the Dispersion' (1:1)!

Contents

Since we are denied an entrance to the teaching of James by means of the questions, 'Who wrote this letter and when and to whom?' we must turn to a different approach by asking, 'Why did he write?' It is no loss to be compelled to do this, for it is always the more profitable question and one, indeed, which opens the Bible to every student. The answer to the question 'When?' almost always requires some specialist knowledge, but the answer to the question 'Why?' is arrived at through study of the book or passage itself.

If we may suppose that this letter was written by the Lord's brother, James, we see from Acts that he was in a privileged position for observing the world-wide church. He presided at representative gatherings (Acts 15:13ff.) and received visiting church leaders (Acts 21:18f.; Gal. 1:19–2:10). From this vantage-point he discerned one common danger among Christians and determined to set it before them urgently and in detail: the danger of knowing the truth but failing to translate it into daily life. To 'hear' the word is one thing; to 'do' it is another (1:22).

James' letter is therefore practical rather than doctrinal.

R. A. Ward in *The New Bible Commentary: Revised* rightly says that it is 'a spiritual corrective and not a theological source-book'. More picturesquely, John Calvin[4] remarks, 'But that he speaks not of the grace of Christ and of faith in him, the reason seems to be this, because he addressed those who had already been rightly taught by others; so that they had need, not so much of doctrine, as of the goads of exhortations.'

We must guard, however, against thinking of James as non-doctrinal. Great biblical truths are present, but in the same way as in, for example, Ephesians 4–6; that is, as the incidentally expressed or clearly implied groundwork of the life that is to be lived. The more one delves into James the more it appears that he is grappling with the great foundational doctrines: the nature of saving faith, the way of sanctification, the nature of the Word of God, the relation of law and grace. But the distinctive value of James is his striking grasp of the integration of truth and life: life cannot be truly lived except through the 'wisdom from above' (1:5; 3:17); the wisdom from above is not truly known until it is translated into action.

Before we attempt to survey the letter in order to elucidate James' exposition of 'truth in action', there is one matter in particular which calls for comment. Is there any conflict between the teaching of James and Paul about justification? Certainly, their words appear irreconcilable: 'If Abraham was justified by works, he has something to boast about, but not before God. For what does the scripture say? "Abraham believed God, and it was reckoned to him as righteousness" ' (Rom. 4:2,3). 'Was not Abraham our father justified by works?' (Jas. 2:21). But it is in fact only verbally that these two Bible writers are in disagreement; the disagreement is, indeed, artificially produced by wrenching James' words out of their context. The full exposition of the position is attemp-

---

[4] J. Calvin, *Commentaries on the Catholic Epistles* (Edinburgh, 1855), p. 278.

ted in the second of the following studies, and for the moment we must be content with the following words:

> 'We are accounted righteous before God, only for the merit of our Lord and Saviour Jesus Christ by Faith, and not for our own works or deservings. . . . Albeit that Good Works, which are the fruits of Faith, and follow after Justification, cannot put away our sins, and endure the severity of God's Judgement; yet are they pleasing and acceptable to God in Christ, and do spring out necessarily of a true and lively Faith; insomuch that by them a lively Faith may be as evidently known as a tree discerned by the fruit.'[5]

The dots in the above quotation divide the special interests and emphases of Paul and James respectively. To Paul the question was, 'How is salvation experienced?' and the answer, 'Not by our works and deservings, but by faith in Jesus.' To James the question was, 'How is true, saving faith to be recognized?' and the answer, 'By the fruits it produces in the believer's life.'

[5]Articles 11 and 12 of The Articles of Religion of the Church of England, to be found in the Book of Common Prayer.

OUTLINE

We must now attempt to give an outline of the contents of James' letter, which, as will be seen, is by no means as disjointed as it appears at first sight. This outline is designed to be used along with a first, quick reading through the letter, so that when we embark on the more detailed studies the reader may be better able to appreciate the place which each individual section occupies in the over-all argument.

1:1 Greeting

The church is dispersed through the world. Later, James will note that there is the sure hope of Christ's coming when Christians will be taken out of the world (5:7) and the days of testing will be over, but at present they are scattered in an alien environment. From this starting-point, James' purpose is to teach how to live out the Christian faith in the world. Hence:

1:2-27 Basic Christian principles

1:2-12 *The tested life.* Their present life of trial affords an opportunity to bring forth the fruits of true faith and thus progress to Christian maturity (2-4). For this, they stand in need of the wisdom God has promised to give (5), bearing in mind that the gift will be given only to the true-hearted (6-8). An illustration (9-11) is used to show how this wisdom gives a right perspective on life's varying circumstances, thus enabling the Christian to win through to the prize (12).

1:13-18 *The new birth*. But in order to persevere to the end, Christians also need true self-knowledge. There remains in the Christian's nature that which actively entices him on the downward path (13-15), notwithstanding the fact that God has brought him to the new birth (16-18). The mere fact of the new birth neither eradicates nor neutralizes man's natural sinful tendencies, but brings the Christian into an internal conflict.

1:19-27 *The Word of God*. How then, in the face of the outward trials of life and the inner conflicts of personal experience, is the Christian to make the progress to maturity spoken of in verses 2-4? How is the new birth of verses 16-18 to become the new life? By receiving (19-21) and obeying (22-25) God's Word. By the Word which He speaks the Father brought about the new birth (18), and by the Word He speaks, received and acted on, He promotes the new life.

There are three distinctive characteristics in this new life (26, 27): a controlled tongue (26), a concern for the needy and helpless (27a) and a life of daily purity, free from worldly taint (27b). Hence:

2:1 – 5:6 Distinctive Christian characteristics

Each of the three characteristics stated in 1:26,27 is now explained in turn: first, concern for the needy (2:1-26; *cf.* verses 6,8,9,13,15,16,25); secondly, the controlled tongue (3:1-18; *cf.* verses 2-10); and thirdly, the life of practical holiness (4:1 – 5:6; *cf.* 'unstained from the world' in 1:27 with 'friendship with the world' in 4:4).

2:1-26 *Concern for the needy*. It is so easy to profess faith in Christ (1) and yet practise un-Christlike standards (2,3) revealing the presence of the deadly sin of the double mind (4). The particular illustration by which James exposes this situation involves adopting attitudes towards other people based on their place in this world's scheme of things, wealth and appearance being the chosen criteria. If Christians act so, they run counter to a basic fact of spiritual experience (5), the general tendency of earthly experience (6,7), and the specific injunction of God's law (8–13).

But is this last matter relevant to the Christian? Does not the gospel of God's free, pardoning grace end the pressure of God's law? James turns to show that God's law remains as the pattern for the outworking of the life of faith (14–26), giving four illustrations (verses 15,16; 18,19; 21–23; 25), to each of which is added the principle it involves (verses 17, 20,24,26).

3:1–18 *Words and wisdom.* It is clear from verses 2–10 that James is now concerned with another of the distinctive characteristics of the Christian life stated in 1:26,27, the control of the tongue. But it is also easy to see how this topic arises out of the foregoing plea for a faith which works. Testimony, speaking and preaching have ever been well established in the forefront of Christian activity, and urged as a primary evidence of the reality of faith in Christ. James enters a caveat on over-hasty embarking upon a speaking vocation (1), and this leads him to a searching examination of the dangerous power of the tongue (2–12).

Having completed this topic, he returns to the implied claim of verse 1. To take on as a teacher is to imply the possession of wisdom. Who is the wise Christian? It is worth remembering that wisdom from God is the basic need if one is to live out the life of faith (1:2–5). But wisdom will make its presence felt not so much in word as in character (13,14), and in the production of those attributes which demonstrate a life lived not by earthly (15,16) but by heavenly wisdom (17,18).

4:1 – 5:6 *Christian constancy.* Comparison of 4:4 with 1:27b shows that James is now determined to expose and call for the erasing of the stains of the world from the Christian. But once again the topic follows naturally from what has immediately preceded. Peaceful relationships are one of the products of the heavenly wisdom (3:14,17) and the soil out of which a life of righteousness grows (3:18). Yet James sees fellowships marred by internal strife (4:1ff.). To acquiesce in this is to settle for 'friendship with the world', of which the inner spring is self-gratification (1–5). This manifests itself in four areas of life, and must be banished from each if the Christian is to be loyal to his faith: pride (Godward; 6–10), defamation (manward; 11,12), presumption (selfward; 13–17), and covetousness (of possessions; 5:1–6).

5:7 – 20 Conclusion: abiding Christian concerns

This is a genuine conclusion. It brings James' teaching full circle. He began by saying that the Christian is marked by perseverance (1:2–4) and prayer (1:5), and he ends on the same notes (5:7–12, 13–18). Further, he outlined the Christian life as involving care for the needy (1:27a; 2:1–26), control of the tongue (1:26; 3:1–18), and pure friendship with God (1:27b; 4:1 – 5:6). He concludes with the same topics in the reverse order: persevering until the Lord's return (5:7–12), the Christian's tongue used in prayer (13–18) and Christian mutual concern (19,20). The treatment of the three cardinal topics is, in these concluding verses, emphatically positive.

1 PROGRESS UNDER TRIAL
1:1 - 27

The Bible is the ever-relevant book. Every part of it began as a message to some particular people at some date in history, but no part exhausts all its meaning upon its first hearers or readers. It remains as a continuing message from God to His people. It is because of this unfathomable aspect of its nature that Stephen, for example, is able to say that Moses at Mount Sinai received oracles from God to give 'to us' (Acts 7:38), thus quietly leaping over 1,200 years of history and asserting the abiding message of God's Word.

James, in a manner characteristic of himself, starts his letter on exactly this note. His address is not to this church or that, in this centre of Christianity or that, or at any particular date, but to the whole church as long as it remains on earth.

1:1 Greeting

1 James, a servant of God and of the Lord Jesus Christ,
To the twelve tribes in the Dispersion:
Greeting.

The origin of James' description of God's people as *the twelve tribes in the Dispersion* must be sought in Exodus 12. Though they had started their sojourn in Egypt by invitation (Gn. 45: 16–20), they ended it as hated and feared immigrants (Ex. 1:8–22). By this time, however, they had developed their characteristic twelve-tribe formation, arising by descent from the twelve sons of Jacob (Ex. 1:1–7). It was as a twelve-tribe people that God redeemed them from Egypt (Ex. 3:7,8; 6:6,7), saving them by means of the blood of the Passover lamb (Ex. 12:13,22,23). So when James addressed *the twelve tribes* he means the total company of God's redeemed people.[1]

For much of their history as recorded in the Bible, the twelve tribes lived in the land which God gave them. Even in this situation they were pressed and oppressed by other nations, and often succumbed to the temptation to conform to pagan ways. These pressures, however, became incomparably more severe when they lost national sovereignty, were deprived of such safeguards and encouragements of true religion as the laws of their own land and the availability of the Temple and its services afforded, and were scattered widespread among the heathen nations. This was *the Dispersion*, which began with the transportation of the conquered people to Assyria (2 Ki. 17:6, 721 BC) and Babylon (2 Ki. 24: 11–16; 25:11–21, 587 BC).

Glancing forward to 5:7–9, we know that James anticipates the day when the Lord will come, the day when, according to Bible teaching, the dispersion of His people in the world will end and we will be gathered to Him for ever.[2] But that day is not yet, and until it comes God's people are in the world, pressed and pressurized to conform, subject to earthly trials and temptations, and in such a setting must learn and be determined to live for God.

How truly, then, we may adapt Stephen's reference to Moses and say that James received oracles from God to give to us!

His opening injunction (verse 2) ought surely to take us by surprise: *Count it all joy . . . when you meet various trials*. At all events this is contrary to natural logic! It is virtually automatic for us, even when we manage to avoid resentment and rebellion in the face of life's adversities, still to see them as

[1]See Introduction, pp. 10-12.
[2]*Cf., e.g.*, Mk. 13:26, 27; Jn. 14:3; 1 Thes. 4:16, 17.

obstacles to spiritual growth. This is not James' view. On the contrary, we are to enter into the difficulties and pressures of life with enthusiasm, for far from being barriers to progress they are God's appointed way ahead. They are, indeed (verse 12), the preliminaries to receiving the great reward.

1:2–12 The life-giving trial

2 Count it all joy, my brethren, when you meet various trials, **³for** you know that the testing of your faith produces steadfastness. **⁴And let steadfastness have its full effect, that you may be perfect and complete, lacking in nothing.**

5 If any of you lacks wisdom, let him ask God, who gives to all men generously and without reproaching, and it will be given him. **⁶But let him ask in faith, with no doubting, for he who doubts is like a wave of the sea that is driven and tossed by the wind. ⁷,⁸For** that person must not suppose that a double-minded man, unstable in all his ways, will receive anything from the Lord.

9 Let the lowly brother boast in his exaltation, **¹⁰and the rich in** his humiliation, because like the flower of the grass he will pass away. **¹¹For the sun rises with its scorching heat and withers the** grass; its flower falls, and its beauty perishes. So will the rich man fade away in the midst of his pursuits.

12 Blessed is the man who endures trial, for when he has stood the test he will receive the crown of life which God has promised to those who love him.

a. Positive teaching (verses 2–4)

When James calls us to count life's trials as joy there is no element of superficiality in his words. It may well be that we are sometimes guilty of saying to each other, 'You must not worry so', when in our hearts we know that there is every reason for anxiety! But James comes to us as one facing, not concealing, the facts. This is the force of the words *for you know* (verse 3) by which he justifies his attitude towards our trials. His appeal is not for the adoption of a superficial gaiety but for a candid assessment of certain truths. He sets before us the following sequence: *faith* meets and bears *the testing* which life's trials bring and the result is *steadfastness* (verse 3), that is a stable, consistent Christian character. Furthermore, when *steadfastness* is allowed to *have its full effect*, *i.e.* when we pursue with determination the pathway of consistent living, the result is the *perfect and complete* Christian, *lacking in nothing*. Note again the sequence, for it is most important: faith, testing, steadfastness, full Christian maturity.

In one sense there is nothing unusual about this: it is just good observation of life. If we were to question a young couple in the earlier days of their friendship, they might well say that they believed they were meant for each other. This, of course, amounts at that point to no more than a matter of tentative opinion. Soon, however, their belief will face tests: the counter-attraction of other possible partners, the experience of those aspects of each other's likes and dislikes which do not automatically blend together, and so forth. But as these testings are successfully endured, the relationship becomes stronger, the mere belief that they are meant to marry becomes a persistent conviction. In their marriage vows they pledge themselves to each other in terms of 'forsaking all other' for life, and in the course of their marriage this is exactly what happens: their minds become irrevocably weaned away from the thought of ever being with anyone else. Thus what began as a tentative belief ends as a fixed, steady, unchangeable character of life.

The same thing can be illustrated in connection with our Christian faith. We believe that God is our Father, but as long as we remain untested on the point our 'belief' falls short of steady conviction. But suppose the day comes, as indeed it does and will, when circumstances seem to mock at our testimony that God is our Father Almighty, Maker of heaven and earth – the cruelty of life denies His fatherliness, His apparent silence calls in question His almightiness, and the sheer, haphazard, meaningless jumble of events challenges the existence of the Creator's ordering hand. If, in that day, we can still stumble to our feet and proclaim, 'Nevertheless "I believe in God the Father Almighty, Maker of heaven and earth" ', faith has passed its test and progressed towards steadfast conviction and full maturity.

Now, that which we have illustrated in two segments of experience James asserts to be a foundation principle of all Christian life. When he speaks of *steadfastness* (verses 3,4), he means consistent living for Christ. He answers the cry of our hearts that we might be less fluctuating in our loyalty, less erratic in our conduct, and his answer is that the trials of life, whether they come from outside through circumstances or through other people, or whether they are the inner temptings to which the same word refers in verses 13,14, are God's designed way forward, for it is only by meeting and passing its tests that faith grows into stable character.

James, however, takes the matter further. He speaks of this procedure as the way to completeness. In other words, he explains the doctrine of sanctification. The objective at the end of this road of testing and steadfastness is *that you may be perfect and complete, lacking in nothing* (verse 4). *Perfect* can best be defined as full maturity of Christian character and life; *complete* and *lacking in nothing* are added by way of positive and negative emphasis, meaning respectively the presence of every single individual thing which is necessary for this perfection, and the absence of any deficiency. Here is the man of God fully fashioned, the complete Christian. But how do we progress towards this goal, for the sequence which James has outlined necessitates that we see the Christian life as one of progress towards the goal of maturity and not as one of arriving at the goal by some great, God-given experience? We progress by means of the testing of faith in the heat of experience, by means of the struggle and fight for consistent living. The testing itself is planned by God to be a life-giving occasion and experience for His people.

b. An assurance and a corrective (verses 5–8)

The connection between verses 4 and 5 is made by the idea of 'lacking'. The forward look to the complete Christian *lacking in nothing* prompts in James' practical mind one factor without which the Christian will never begin to move forward to that great goal. Therefore he proceeds: *If any of you lacks wisdom.*

Wisdom has a double significance: it holds together both the possession of knowledge and the ability to make right decisions. James may therefore have in mind the person who doubts if the way to sanctification outlined in verses 2–4 is correct. He certainly has in mind the person who is uncertain how to behave in the trials and troubles of life so as to make headway for God. To each alike James says, *If any of you lacks wisdom, let him ask God* (verse 5). This is intended to give us a basic assurance of God's own readiness to lead us forward. We need hold back neither for lack of conviction that this is the biblical way of sanctification (though, of course, it is) nor for lack of perception of which way to turn in the maze of life. We ask for wisdom and God gives it.

God's unclouded desire for our spiritual progress, expressed in verse 5, can be summed up in three words: simplicity, availability, liberality. The simplicity is that of prayer: all we need do is *ask*. The availability is that of God Himself: we do not have to search for a friend, or wait for a more experienced Christian to come our way, or depend on a letter going and a reply returning. We turn to the ever-present God, approaching Him through the ever-open door of intercession. The liberality is that which excludes no-one, for God *gives to all men*. Indeed, He ever goes beyond what is required, for He gives *generously*, and even then He leaves the door of request wide open, for He gives *without reproaching*, not holding it against us that we come so often, or that we frequently trade upon His goodness, or that we have squandered or failed to appreciate His earlier gifts.

James, however, knows our hearts all too well! It is both interesting and humbling to ask why the particular truths given in verses 6–8 follow on the truths of verse 5. The answer is this: verse 5 holds up before us the unquestioned sincerity of God, who desires our progress and who will not withhold from us the wisdom we need if we are to go forward with Him; verses 6–8 raise the matter of our sincerity. Do we want whole-heartedly to go forward with God? Are we all of a piece in our attitude to Him? Or are we keeping the door open for the world? Are we trying to have a foot in each camp? God's mind is clear; are we 'double-minded'?

The 'doubting' which mars the purity of faith can be clearly understood in the light of James' illustration. The *wave* is caught in the conflicting impulses of tide and wind, so that while it tends in one direction it is whipped in another. Thus Christians can be caught in the cross-currents of life, just as the Lord Jesus speaks (using another metaphor) of 'the cares of the world, and the delight in riches, and the desire for other things' which choke the Word (Mk. 4:19). Thus the element of 'doubt'[3] bedevils our relationship with God, and we become the man of verse 8, *double-minded*, or, as we might well translate it, two-faced with God. Without a steady gaze upon God there can be no stability in the outward life. Such a person 'never can keep a steady course' (NEB), for the wisdom from on high is withheld from him.

c. An illustration (verses 9-11)

James moves on now from the assurance that God will lead us forward by His gift of wisdom to an illustration. Here are two of the contrasting situations of life, poverty and wealth,

[3]The verb does not necessarily have a bad meaning. It is frequently used in the proper sense of 'to discriminate', 'to judge as between good and evil'; but from this it developed, as here in James, the meaning 'to be in two minds'.

and each is liable to move a person off course. Poverty can move a person from inflexible loyalty to God simply through the sheer difficulty of living. Wealth can seduce a man's mind from undeviating loyalty to God by putting up the counter-attraction of the things of the world. In these two contrasting circumstances, therefore, we see a sample of the trials of life, and it is James' purpose to show us how the wisdom that God gives enables people to face them and win through.

The *lowly brother*, instructed by the wisdom of God, does not see the poverty of his circumstances but the wealth of glory that is his in Christ (verse 9). The rich brother (verse 10) sees *his humiliation* not because he had to come low before the cross in order to become a Christian (though that in itself is true), but because the wisdom that comes from above enables him to see his wealth in its true colours. He sees it (verse 10b) as something that is as transient, as the flower, or the grass that easily withers. He sees it (verse 11a) as something that utterly depends upon the favour of circumstances: the sun and the scorching wind arise and wither the grass. He sees it (verse 11b) as something that soon fades away from its promised glory: *its flower falls, and its beauty perishes*. He sees his wealth in those colours because wisdom from on high has given him the eyes so to see it.

Thus wisdom enables men to face the circumstances of life and to go on with God. We may put it this way in the light of the examples given: wisdom enables us to see heaven clearly, and to see earth clearly. The poor man is enabled to go on with God in spite of the adverse circumstances of poverty because the wisdom from on high has opened the glories of heaven to him, and he counts them richer than all the trials of earth. And the rich man is enabled to go on with God in spite of the snares and enticements of wealth, because wisdom from on high has opened his eyes to the real state of earthly things, how perishable they are, how unsatisfactory they are in the long run. Wisdom opens the eyes both to the glories of heaven and to the hollownesses of earth. Therefore the wisdom which God gives enables us in all circumstances to go on with Him.

d. A promise (verse 12)

Now James in every sense puts the crown on the whole sequence of his teaching by a concluding promise. He has shown us God's way forward; now we see how God is waiting at the end of this process with a crown to give to the victorious Christian. Faith, the test, victory, and on to maturity and the crown from the hand of God! God's divinely-given crown entices the Christian graciously on the road of conflict right through to the place of maturity and the heavenly reward.

In the divine planning of our circumstances, testing and trial is a life-giving experience. The trials are not unnatural things, nor obstacles to spiritual growth. They are God's appointed way forward.

1:13 – 18 The life-giving God

13 Let no one say when he is tempted, 'I am tempted by God'; for God cannot be tempted with evil and he himself tempts no one; ¹⁴but each person is tempted when he is lured and enticed by his own desire. ¹⁵Then desire when it has conceived gives birth to sin; and sin when it is full-grown brings forth death.

16 Do not be deceived, my beloved brethren. ¹⁷Every good endowment and every perfect gift is from above, coming down from the Father of lights with whom there is no variation or shadow due to change. ¹⁸Of his own will he brought us forth by the word of truth that we should be a kind of first fruits of his creatures.

The God who gives wisdom to His tested people is also the God who gives them life. In stating and explaining this, the second of his basic Christian principles, James both links it with what has preceded and gives it a characteristically practical setting.

27

Twice already he has turned our attention from life's testing circumstances to the state of our own inner hearts and minds. First, he did this (verse 5–8) by his frank reminder that it is possible to be in two minds whether to walk the way of faith or not. Secondly, at the end of verse 12, he introduced the thought that *the crown of life* has been *promised* by God *to those who love him*. Clearly this is crucial. If we really loved God, we would not be bothered with this problem of being two-faced. We would look up to God in pure, unmixed devotion, and we would say to Him, 'I want absolutely nothing but to go on with You and Your way. Will You give me wisdom?' We would not be troubled by being like the surging sea, because our hearts would be fixed upon Him. Once more James has his finger on the spot so far as our problems are concerned. There is more to life than outward trials. Comparison of RSV with the older translations shows that very wisely at this point it makes a significant change in translation. Up to verse 12, it uses the word 'trial'; from verse 12 onwards it uses the word 'temptation'. There is more to life than the outward trials. Indeed on many occasions we could stand the outward trials if it was not for the inner snares and temptations that seem to speak to us and to attract us in our own hearts.

And to this practical truth James now turns his attention. He makes first of all (verses 13–16) a vital distinction and then (verses 17, 18) states a vital truth.

a. A vital distinction (verses 13–16)

In a word, the distinction is this: God uses the testings of circumstances to lead us forward from faith to steadfastness and maturity, but it is not God's voice that tempts us to give up and go the way of self-pleasing.

The origin of temptation is explained in verses 13,14. God, we are told, is of such unmixed holiness that He *cannot be tempted with evil,* and of such unmixed goodness that *he himself tempts no one.* Therefore the voice which says, 'Give up, go the way of sin and self-pleasing, disobey God', cannot come from Him. It is impossible for the holy One to be enticed so as to plot to hurt us like this, and to do so would contradict His essential goodness. The voice we hear is our own, the voice of our fallen nature. *Desire* does not, of course, necessarily imply a longing for something sinful, and in this connection we need to beware of the translation 'lust' familiar to users of the older versions (AV, RV). We may simply recall the words of Jesus already quoted about 'desire for other things'. So often even the allowable desires of our hearts tend to draw us away from a consistent walk with God.

Falling into temptation is never an isolated act. It has a background in our hearts, and it has consequences, as James now makes clear, outlining in verses 15,16 the course of temptation. *Desire* signifies the entertaining in the mind and emotions of some action. When the thought passes over into the deed it becomes *sin*, and the end result of the process is *death.* We can best understand what death means in this context if we consider for a moment our ability to form habits, good and bad. It all begins when some action or experience is presented to our minds as attractive and rewarding. The thought fathers the deed. Soon desire rekindles, and the fact of having performed the act once (whether it is a good or bad act does not matter) predisposes the mind towards repetition. Presently repetition becomes the rule and a habit is formed, but precisely at what point occasional indulgence became a fixed way of life, a part of our character, would be impossible to say. Yet there was such a point: a point beyond which the giving up of the habit became impossible. In this way we may try to understand the use of the idea of death, for death is *par excellence* the point of no return. Just as the dead have no ability to return to life, so the sinner has no ability to break off his sin, divest himself of his sinful nature and return to God.

James faithfully raises up for us a grim warning. Every sin and all sinful indulgence partakes of a fixed process, beginning with the thought in the mind and ending in death. It is parallel to the process by which faith grows, through weathering its storms, to steadfastness, maturity and the crown of life. The one process ends in life, the other in death, and James is insistent that we should not be deceived on this point (verse 16[4]).

It will be seen, then, that we are in something of a dilemma. If the crown is given to the man who loves God (verse 12), and yet it is from the heart with which we are to love God that the enticement to sin comes, how can we ever gain the crown?

b. A vital truth (verses 17, 18)

If we are to appreciate the full force of the truth which James now sets before us, we must begin by seeing how exactly he matches and balances what he has pressed home in the immediately preceding verses. Verse 17 resumes the topic of verse 13. There we saw the unmixed holiness and goodness of God who can neither be attracted by nor be the source of evil; now we see His unmixed benevolence towards us. Having denied that He can do us harm, James now asserts that He does us only good. The goodness of God to us is first noted as unquestionable: the gifts themselves are *good*, *i.e.* lovely, pleasant and designed to bring benefit, and *perfect*, *i.e.* lacking nothing to make them complete and suited to the occasion. And the Giver is the *Father of lights*, the God from whom all darkness such as might conceal an ulterior motive is absent. Secondly, His goodness is unvarying for in God

---

[4]Verse 16 may, of course, be attached to verses 17ff., as in RSV. If so, it calls us to be clear-headed that temptation to sin cannot come from God (but must come from our own nature). It is a matter of personal preference which way it is to be taken.

there is no variation or shadow due to change. The basis of this expression is possibly the observation that the sun, in changing its position in the heavens, and in shining with varying strength, casts now one shadow and now another. Hence, we read in NEB, 'No play of passing shadows'. 'His goodness', says Mitton, 'is not occasional or fitful, but unceasing and unfading, steady and persistent.'[5]

This truth leads us straight into verse 18: the crowning proof of God's perfect goodness is the new birth. But observe how verse 18 balances verses 14,15. We are not left to the mercy of the old nature, enticing, death-bound. God has brought us to the new birth; a new nature lives within us. We are taught three things about this new birth: its ground, its means and its purpose.

The ground of the new birth was God's will. The words *his own will* express exactly the correct emphasis. This was something God Himself decided upon. He did not act under pressure from us or others; He took no-one into His confidence, nor did He seek advice on the point. The new birth was wholly and solely the product of His free, sovereign, uncompelled will.[6] The means used by God to accomplish His gracious purpose in us was *the word of truth, i.e.* God's creative Word. Just as in the beginning 'God said, "Let there be light"; and there was light',[7] so, at the moment He appointed for our new birth, He said, 'Let there be life, and there was life.' Thirdly, the purpose of God in bringing us to the new birth was *that we should be a kind of first fruits of his creatures.* Here James takes up one of those illustrative Old Testament ideas which were so dear to him. The first of the

[5]C. L. Mitton, *The Epistle of James* (London, 1966). R. V. G. Tasker, *The General Epistle of James* (London, 1956), notes that the Greek used in this expression 'implies that there is no possibility of any such change'.
[6]*Cf.* Jn. 1:12, 13; 3:1–8; Tit. 3:4–7. Even the repentance and faith whereby we enter consciously into the new life in Christ are given and created in us by God. *E.g.* Rom. 10:17; Eph. 2:8; 2 Tim. 2:25.
[7]Gn. 1:3; Ps. 33:6,9; 2 Cor. 4:6; 1 Pet. 1:23–25.

produce was given to God to become His sole possession and to partake of His holiness (*cf.* Je. 2:2,3). The purpose of the new birth was that we should be God's very own, and be holy as He is.[8]

1:19–27 The life-giving Word

19 Know this, my beloved brethren. Let every man be quick to hear, slow to speak, slow to anger, [20]for the anger of man does not work the righteousness of God. [21]Therefore put away all filthiness and rank growth of wickedness and receive with meekness the implanted word, which is able to save your souls.

[22]But be doers of the word, and not hearers only, deceiving yourselves. [23]For if any one is a hearer of the word and not a doer, he is like a man who observes his natural face in a mirror; [24]for he observes himself and goes away and at once forgets what he was like. [25]But he who looks into the perfect law, the law of liberty, and perseveres, being no hearer that forgets but a doer that acts, he shall be blessed in his doing.

26 If any one thinks he is religious, and does not bridle his tongue but deceives his heart, this man's religion is vain. [27]Religion that is pure and undefiled before God and the Father is this: to visit orphans and widows in their affliction, and to keep oneself unstained from the world.

Reviewing James' teaching so far we may say that he started by making us look about us at life's trials, insisting that they are designed by God to be the means of our spiritual growth, provided that we meet them in the light of God-given wisdom (verses 2–5). Then he turned our gaze in, so that we might see the lurking enemy of our own old nature ever-active in enticement to sin. And alongside that he placed the reality of the new birth, God's life in us, purposing our holiness (verses 13–18).

From each of these aspects of his teaching a question arises. How does God communicate His wisdom to us? And along what lines and by what means does the new birth develop into the new life?

[8]*Cf.* Lv. 19:2; Dt. 14:1,2; Mt. 5:48; 1 Pet. 1:14–17.

Both these questions are answered in verses 19–27, but, of course, it is the second which more immediately gives rise to this third section of James' statement of basic Christian principles. The new birth leaves the Christian in a condition of inner division. To the same person James can say *each person is tempted when he is lured and enticed by his own desire* (verse 14), and *of his own will he brought us forth* (verse 18). The new life is challenged and resisted, and there is an inevitable element of conflict created by the gift of the new birth. We need, therefore, to be told what is the way of growth, the way of victory.

To all these questions James' straightforward answer is the Word of God.[9]

a. Hearing God's Word (verses 19,20)

In verse 19 the AV reads 'Wherefore', which, though it is a wrong translation, nevertheless gives us the correct clue to the connection between this verse and what has gone before. James directs our gaze back to the fact of the new birth and then forward to the consequences which should follow if we are to grow up. The correct translation is: 'You know this' (or, 'Know this'), '. . . but . . .'. It is the one thing to know about new birth; 'but' it is another to know the way of progress from infancy to adult life. If, however, this growth is to come to pass, then *Let every man be quick to hear.* The first clue to spiritual growth is to hear the Word of God, and this makes sense. It is a life-giving Word. It was by this Word that He brought us to the new birth, and we grow in the Christian

[9]We have every ground for saying that by *the word* which Christians are to receive (verse 21) and do (verse 22) James would mean the teaching of God given in the holy Scriptures and preached in the apostolic gospel. His constant references to the Old Testament show its currency among his readers. *Cf.* Timothy's possession of both the apostolic teaching and the 'sacred writings', together constituting 'all scripture', 2 Tim. 3:15,16.

life by continuing to pay heed to the same Word which gave us life to start with.

There are, however, hindrances to this fruitful 'hearing' of God's Word (verses 19b,20), in particular talking and anger. Nothing is more certain than that we will not hear God's Word if we are doing all the talking! So be swift to hear and slow to speak and above all, do not let your tongue run away with you. *Be slow to anger*, because it is not man's hot zeal that accomplishes God's righteous purposes. James is fearfully strong against the sins of speech, as we shall see more and more. He brings it in here very deliberately. He could have mentioned a hundred-and-one things that keep us from listening to the Word of God, but he says, 'Watch specially your tongue. Keep your tongue under control in the interests of listening, of being swift to hear.' We must *hear* the Word of God.

b. Receiving God's Word (verse 21)

Because the Word which God speaks is the means of life, the Christian must be a great listener, but there is more to it than mere listening; there is also receiving. James is here calling to mind the Parable of the Sower. The Sower sows the seed; He does the planting. But if there is to be fruit from the planting, the seed must be received into an honest and good heart (*cf*. Lk. 8:15). As James sees it, this involves two things: weeding and sowing. One does not need to be an experienced gardener to know that the ground must be cleared to receive seed, and also that if ground is cleared and then left unsown the weeds return overnight. This is morally and spiritually true also: it is the process of weeding out sin and planting in the Word of God.

All filthiness, as it stands in our text, could link back with the revelation of the enticing sinfulness of the heart in verse 14. Wherever sin shows its presence it must be banished. But it is more likely that James has an immediate reference to the foregoing sins of speech, and that the translation should be 'all such filthiness'. This would certainly accord with James' view of the seriousness of sins of speech, and it is a salutary reminder to us that something to which we pay but small heed – the slip of the tongue, the lightly spoken word, the flash of anger, the hot outburst – the scripture does not hesitate to call *filthiness*.

It is not so easy to decide the precise meaning of the words translated *rank growth of wickedness* (*cf.* NEB, 'the malice which hurries to excess'). If this is correct, then James is adding urgency to his call to be busy rooting out sin by reminding us that sin is a rampant growth. It is possible, however, that the phrase means something like 'every last trace of wickedness',[1] and that the purpose is to inculcate in us an unrelenting hostility towards sin, an intolerance towards it even in the smallest surviving manifestation.

On the other hand, we are to *receive with meekness*, that is, with glad, submissive obedience, whatever the Word of God says to us, treating it as the truth by which we live. And what do we receive when we receive the Word? We receive spiritual vitality because it *is able to save your souls*. It is the life-giving Word, and the business of hoeing out sin and planting in the Word of God is in fact a deliberate taking into our lives of fresh spiritual dynamic which can bring us on in vital fashion to maturity. We must receive the Word of God.

c. Obeying God's Word (verses 22–27)

There is a third aspect of our relationship to the Word of God if we are to grow up in Christ. It is summed up in the

---

[1] *Cf.* Tasker. Mitton also holds this view: the word means 'that which survives' or 'the remainder'. Calvin remarks, 'Still some remnants of the old man ever abide in us.'

single word *doers* (verse 22). As he opens up this truth to us, James teaches us three distinct things: the nature of disobedience (verses 22–24), the pathway of obedience (verse 25), and the marks of the true Christian (verses 26, 27).

Turning to the first of these, it is James' insistence that there is no excuse for being a second-rate Christian. This comes out in the word (verse 22) translated *deceiving yourselves*. The meaning would be more accurately expressed by 'excusing yourselves', that is, making up what appear to be good reasons for not obeying God's Word. As it is used in the New Testament (*e.g.* Col. 2:4) it conveys the notion of reasons which have an air of correctness but actually have no substance at all. In this way, there are a variety of reasons (so-called) whereby we side-step the obligation of obeying God's Word, but James will not have it so. Every such 'reason' is a mere excuse, and to live below the level of obedience is inexcusable. That is why he uses the illustration of a person who looks in a mirror and then forgets. Such a person might say, for example, 'Oh, my hair needs combing!' but then he goes away and does nothing about it. The very fact of having looked in a mirror leaves him without excuse. Equally, we have no excuse for being second-rate Christians because, coming to the Word of God, we come to the place where God speaks the Word which both commands and empowers, the Word which can lift us up, on the basis of the new birth, into new realms of Christian living.

Secondly (verse 25), there is the pathway of obedience. There are two descriptions here of the Word of God. It is *law, i.e.* it is the rule of life; and as the rule of life for us it is *perfect*, perfectly suited to our nature and situation. The second description is that it is the law of *liberty, i.e.* coming into our lives with all its ruling power, it also liberates. When we come into bondage to the Word of God we come into freedom, because this Word liberates from the lustful pull of our own nature, and brings us on, via the pathway of hard obedience, into new realms of living for God. It is the law of liberty.

If the Word of God is to exercise this liberating power in our lives, there are two requirements which we must fulfil. James speaks in this verse of 'looking into' the law and 'persevering' in it. The Scriptures neither reveal their directives nor make available their power to the casual, superficial and spasmodic reader. It is interesting to note that the verb 'to look into' is found in John 20:5 and describes how Peter and the other disciple first looked into the empty tomb. One can readily believe that this was no casual glance. They had been forewarned that the body of Jesus was not there, and it is surely not an excessive use of the imagination to understand that they intended to miss nothing which the tomb might reveal to them about Jesus and the still mysterious events of that early morning. At all events, such must surely be our approach to God's Word.

There is also the element of perseverance. James uses a word closely related to Paul's command to Timothy to 'continue' in the apostolic teaching and the sacred writings (2 Tim. 3:14). Any difference in meaning between them can be expressed by saying that Paul's word tends to signify staying in a place, taking up one's abode, while James' word means staying beside a person, cultivating a companionship. Such a matter is not the work of one meeting or of one day, but of a lifetime. It is seen as clearly as it can be in the deep and pervasive matching of lives, personalities and thoughts which emerges in the course of a happy marriage, and this is certainly what James is teaching about entering into a fruitful and empowering relationship with the holy Scriptures.

Finally, we come to the marks of the true Christian (verses 26, 27). In this last section James has first of all called on us to hear the Word of God (verse 19). Next, if our hearing is to be genuine, he instructed us to receive it (verse 21), to hide it away in our hearts. But, in addition, if our receiving is genuine, then it will be seen outwardly in doing the Word (verses 22f.). Finally he comes to this, that if our doing of the Word is genuine, it will show in our lives by certain clear distinguishing marks (verses 26,27), the lines of genuine obedience: a controlled tongue; caring love for the helpless; and holy separation from all defilements of the world.

These are not accidental marks. Consider them in turn. First, a controlled tongue. By what means did we come to the new birth? 'By the word of truth' (verse 18). Our heavenly Father spoke to us. He said, 'Let there be light', and there was light. Should not therefore the children of this God who speaks the Word of truth be known by the Word of truth upon their lips and by a controlled tongue that is rigidly harnessed to the Word of truth? If He is a great Speaker should not we match Him in the things we say?

Secondly, caring love for the helpless is not an accidental or optional manifestation of the new nature but part of its essence. When Jesus came to the city of Nain and met the funeral of the orphan boy and saw the tearful bereft widowed mother, and when He restored the orphan and comforted the widow, people said, 'God has visited his people!' (Lk. 7:11–16). How right they were, for it was a clear part of their Old Testament heritage to think of their God as the Father of the fatherless and the Defender of the widow's cause (*e.g.* Pss. 10:14; 68:5). But for us there is an additional reason why we should reveal ourselves as the children of such a Father by copying His works: in bringing us forth by the Word of truth and making us His children, He has given a paramount display of His concern for the helpless and needy. The very new birth itself has its origin in God's caring love for the desolate. Is it not, therefore, essentially required of those who profess the new birth that they show their Father's likeness?

Finally, we saw (verse 18) that the Father brought us to

the new birth in order that we might be 'first fruits' and the implication of this is that we are to be His holy possession. Consequently, when James marks the Christian as one who is to keep himself *unstained from the world*, once more he is not demanding some external or artificial characteristic but one which belongs naturally with what God has done and planned for us.

The explanation and exposition of these three marks of Christian living need not concern us now, for, as we saw in the synopsis of the letter given in the Outline (pages 15 – 18), James' great purpose is to spell out these topics in detail in the following chapters. He has now reached his first objective – to show what are the main lines of Christian obedient living, and to show the principles on which such a life can be lived – and we can sum up the message of his first chapter as follows: the life of Christian maturity is something for which we must battle and fight in the midst of outward pressures and inward temptations. In this battle we have the reassurance that God has given us new life, and that this life is powerfully ours as we hear, receive and obey God's Word. The life of sanctification is the life of obedience.

2 THE LAW OF GOD AND THE LIFE OF FAITH
2:1 - 26

A single topic dominates the second chapter of James' letter: loving concern for the needy. It appears in verse 2 in an illustration by which he shows that it is possible for Christians to judge others at face value, based on worldly standards of estimation, and that when this happens there is an inevitable failure to pay proper regard to the poor, the lowly, the needy. This is the *partiality* of which he complains (verse 1). He resumes the topic in verse 8, now quoting God's *royal law*, and thus making failure in due regard for the needy a primary sin of disobedience. Another illustration (verse 15) points to a professed faith which is empty of real content, devoid of its proper nature as faith: a so-called faith which produces no fruit of practical compassion. Finally, the chapter ends by recalling the history of Rahab (verse 25). It is James' intention to show how real her faith was, and in order to do this he makes no appeal to her marvellous recorded testimony (*cf.* Jos. 2:9–11), but only to the fact that *she received the messengers:* here were people in particular need and danger, and Rahab reached out, at great risk to herself, and took them into her own home.

James, therefore, is beginning his elaboration of the distinctive characteristics of the Christian life on which he ended the first section of his letter (1:26–28). Since the structure of the letter is so often a puzzle to the reader, it may be well to ask here why he begins with concern for the needy, the second of the marks mentioned in 1:26–28, instead of with the first, the controlled tongue. In chapter 1 James is tackling the struggle for Christian living, and it may be that in his practical way he lists the distinguishing marks of the Christian life in the order in which the pressures of daily life make us face them: first, the struggle with ourselves, at the centre of which James places the battle for the pure tongue; secondly, to live for Christ in relation to other people; and thirdly, over-arching all, the call to please our Father in all things by purity from worldly defilements.

When James begins his more systematic treatment of these topics, however, he does a very interesting thing: he looks back beyond 1:26–28 to 1:18, the verse in which he outlined how we came to be Christians at all. The primary factor was the will of God, and anticipating 2:5 we see how that dictates the primary importance of the subject of care for the needy: we would not be Christians at all were it not the very nature of God, expressed in His choice of us, to concern Himself with the helpless. It must therefore be our first distinguishing mark. The Father gave expression to His choice of us by speaking the word of new creation (1:18), and so we must model ourselves on Him and be known by our speech (3:1ff.). Thirdly, God chose us with the purpose of holiness (1:18), and that life of separation to Him must be followed through with determination in all the great areas of experience (4:1 – 5:6). God's plan of salvation is thus to be mirrored in the life of those whom He has willed to be His new-born children.

All this would make the contents of chapter 2 of surpassing importance, but James makes even further demands on our attention to our concern for the needy by the specific setting he gives it in the life of faith to which the Christian is called. He begins by referring to holding *the faith of our Lord Jesus Christ* (verse 1), and ends with a sustained examination of what faith means (verses 14–26). There are, as we shall see, three sections in this chapter, and each contains two elements: some aspect of the life of faith, and an insistence on care for the needy. What does this mean but that if we sidestep our responsibility to the poor, the helpless, the outcast, we are not making a marginal error but failing in the life of faith itself. We shall try to make this clear by discussing all the material in this chapter in terms of faith and its divinely intended outworking.

2:1 – 7 The life of imitation

1 My brethren, show no partiality as you hold the faith of our Lord Jesus Christ, the Lord of glory. [2]For if a man with gold rings and in fine clothing comes into your assembly, and a poor man in shabby clothing also comes in, [3]and you pay attention to the one who wears the fine clothing and say, 'Have a seat here, please,' while you say to the poor man, 'Stand there,' or 'Sit at my feet,' [4]have you not made distinctions among yourselves, and become judges with evil thoughts ? [5]Listen, my beloved brethren. Has not God chosen those who are poor in the world to be rich in faith and heirs of the kingdom which he has promised to those who love him ? [6]But you have dishonoured the poor man. Is it not the rich who oppress you, is it not they who drag you into court ? [7]Is it not they who blaspheme that honourable name by which you are called ?

The illustration in verses 2,3 is brought to a point in verse 4. Here the NEB expresses the meaning exactly: 'Do you not see that you are inconsistent and judge by false standards?'[1] We are, as a matter of fact, dealing with the same word as in 1:6, *doubting*, which, as we saw there, means unable to adopt a stable point of view, now going this way, now that, facing both ways, two-faced with God. James has no objection to make against true Christian discrimination: it is no mark of godliness to be gullible! But he does object to the jostling of

---

[1]RSV 'make distinctions' presumably looks back to the falsely-drawn distinction between rich and poor in the preceding illustration, but it is not really 'making distinctions' that is called in question, but making false distinctions. RV 'divided in your own mind' catches, as it so often does, exactly the correct nuance.

two irreconcilable standards, God's and the world's, in the same person, who on the one hand professes faith in the Lord Jesus, and on the other goes the way of the world in disregard of the poor and cultivation of the rich.

a. The glory of Jesus (verses 1–4)

James calls Jesus *the Lord of glory*. This may simply mean 'the glorious Lord', or more strikingly 'the Lord, who is the Glory'.[2] At all events the point of the description is surely this, that to judge by earthly standards is to fail to see that the glory of Jesus, or the glory of God revealed in Jesus, is the true criterion for life's decisions.

What are we to understand by the glory of Jesus? It means either or both of two things. One is this: the value which God places on lowliness. How did Jesus become the Lord of glory? It was because He made Himself of no reputation, took upon Himself the form of a servant and was made in the likeness of man, humbled Himself, and carried His obedience to God even to the point of death, and that the death of the cross. 'Therefore God has highly exalted him and bestowed on him the name which is above every name' (Phil. 2: 7–11). When we fill our eyes with the Lord Jesus in glory we are automatically saying to ourselves, 'Now we see the estimate which God places on lowliness: He is the Lord of glory, because He went down and took the lowest place.'

Alternatively, or perhaps as well, we may look at it this way: the readiness of Jesus to identify Himself with man in his lowliness is the reason why He is now the Lord of glory. He is crowned with glory and honour because of the suffering of death (Heb. 2:9); because He identified Himself with us

[2]*Cf.* Mitton, *op. cit.* Mitton fails to follow through this suggestion, but it is clearly pertinent to what he has just said about the character of God showing itself in Christ (*e.g.* 2 Cor. 4:6) and providing a basis for Christian ethics. To fall short of Him is to recede from the glory.

in the lowest depths of our lost estate, 'the highest place that heaven affords is His, is His by right'. It was at this point that Jesus both began and ended His ministry. When John demurred about baptizing Him, Jesus replied, 'Thus it is fitting for us to fulfil all righteousness' (Mt. 3:15). We may understand Him to have meant, 'It is in this way that we are to fulfil God's righteous plan' – a sense which the word 'righteousness' bears in some Old Testament contexts.[3] John's baptism was for penitents, and it signified remission of sins. It is clear that those who saw Jesus come (*cf.* Lk. 3:21) must have understood that He was repenting and seeking forgiveness, as they were. John alone of men knew otherwise.

God's righteous plan, then, was for Jesus, the sinless One, to identify Himself with, and be taken as numbered with, sinners. And what His baptism commenced His cross completed. If we do not identify ourselves with Him in His concern for the poor and needy, how can we claim to be reposing faith in Him as Lord of glory? If we do truly believe in Him, must we not imitate Him?

b. The mind of God (verses 5,6a)

The second element in a true standard of judgment is that failure to care for the needy is failure to reflect the mind of God as revealed in our salvation.

The whole story of our salvation is in verse 5: past, present, and future. If we look in Scripture for the past of our salvation, we find it written: God chose. That was when our salvation began. Its beginning antedated the moment of conversion, for Jesus said, 'You did not choose me, but I chose you' (Jn. 15:16). In saying this, He did not mean to deny or to deride that well-remembered moment in many an individual's experience when faith first consciously laid hold on Jesus as Saviour. He meant that what made our choice poss-

[3] *E.g.* Is. 41:2 (RV); 42:6.

ible and meaningful was the fact that He had already chosen us long before. Again, the beginning of our salvation ante-dated the creation itself, for He (the Father) 'chose us in him (Christ) before the foundation of the world' (Eph. 1:4). Our salvation is thus rooted in the mind, determination and active choice of God, long before we knew or thought about Him (*cf.* Jas. 1:18).

The present of our salvation is also in verse 5, for it says *rich in faith . . . those who love him.* Those whom God chose He also brought to faith – that faith which is the gift of God that we might believe in Him (Eph. 2:8) – and to exercise towards Him that love which the Holy Spirit prompts when He first sheds abroad God's love for us in our hearts (Rom. 5:5), so that we love Him because He first loved us (1 Jn. 4: 19). The present inheritance of the saved believer is to believe in God and to love Him.

And the future of our salvation is in this verse, for we read here of the kingdom which He has promised, and we look forward to the glory that is yet to be when His servants shall serve Him and shall see His face (Rev. 22: 3,4). Here is the greatness of our salvation; but it began in the mind of God. It began when God cast His mind in a certain direction and chose the poor of this world, for as the apostle Paul reminds us, in the working out of salvation, 'not many of you were wise according to worldly standards, not many were powerful, not many were of noble birth; but God chose what is foolish in the world . . . God chose what is weak . . . God chose what is low and despised . . . even things that are not . . .' (1 Cor. 1: 26–29). Salvation reveals the mind of God. God is concerned for the neglected and the abased and the worthless; and if we make judgments on people based on earthly standards we are contradicting the mind of God as revealed in our salvation.

Furthermore, if we fail to appreciate the needy and to identify with them, then there is a failure to express our own new position in Christ.

When James speaks here of the oppressive rich it is likely enough that he is commenting directly on a notable feature of the contemporary church,[4] but apart from this possibility his words form a true generalization on church history, and point up the absurdity, therefore, of Christians being misled by worldly glitter into any exaltation of the wealthy as such.

Within this general truth, however, James enshrines an abiding truth, that the real sting of persecution is not that it comes from the rich or any other group, nor that Christians are dragged into court, but that blasphemy is offered to *that honourable name by which you are called* (verse 7). In this way he brings before the Christian who might be tempted to follow the attractiveness of wealth and despise the needy the criterion of his own new position in Christ: that Christ as a Bridegroom has espoused us to Himself and has given us His name in marriage. Behind this illustrative mode of viewing our relationship to the Lord there probably lies the fact of Christian baptism. The words could well be translated 'the honoured name which was invoked over you' or (NEB) 'the honoured name by which God has claimed you'. This would reflect the inner heart of the baptismal symbol, baptism into the name of the Father and the Son and the Holy Spirit. Thus He symbolically gives us His name and seals to us the divine nature and all the promises which accompany salvation. But the divine nature thus symbolically bestowed, whether we hold to the fact of baptism or the concept of the marriage of Christ and His church, is the nature of the Lord of glory who came to His throne by way of and by means of identifying Himself with the poor and needy. James, there-

[4]*Cf.* in the earliest days of church history, Acts 4:1–3 (opposition from leaders); 13: 50 (leading men); 16:19; 19:23ff. (commercial interests).

fore, is yet again asserting that the life of faith in this Lord is the life of imitating His way of seeing and doing things, and we put our living of that life in jeopardy if we fail to do what He did, taking it as a deliberate policy to identify with and rescue the rejects of this world.

2:8–13 The life of obedience

8 If you really fulfil the royal law, according to the scripture, 'You shall love your neighbour as yourself,' you do well. ⁹But if you show partiality, you commit sin, and are convicted by the law as transgressors. ¹⁰For whoever keeps the whole law but fails in one point has become guilty of all of it. ¹¹For he who said, 'Do not commit adultery,' said also, 'Do not kill.' If you do not commit adultery but do kill, you have become a transgressor of the law. ¹²So speak and so act as those who are to be judged under the law of liberty. ¹³For judgment is without mercy to one who has shown no mercy; yet mercy triumphs over judgment.

The connection of verses 8ff. with the preceding teaching will be seen more clearly if we alter the order of words in RSV and read, not *If you really fulfil*, but Really, if you fulfil'. James' purpose appears to be to lift the subject out of the realm of the immediately foregoing illustration into the realm of positive truth. We might paraphrase, 'What it comes to is this: keep the royal law.' Christian behaviour is not to be confined, in this matter, to any tendency towards undue regard for the rich as such compared with the poor as such. It is a matter of guarding against *partiality* (verse 9) in every human situation, and this is catered for by a clear precept of God's law, given for our obedience.

Concerning this, James says three things:

a. The Christian is subject to the royal law[5] (verses 8,9)

He assumes our obligation to the law of God, and he singles

[5]The description of the royal law as being *according to the scripture* refers to Lv. 19:15,18; cf. Mt. 5:43f.; 19:19; 22:39; Rom. 13:9; Gal. 5 : 14.

out a particular law which he calls royal. Maybe he calls it the royal law because it is the law of the kingdom of God: James has just reminded us that, as part of our salvation, we have been ushered into membership of the kingdom (verse 5) and he may now mean that as members we are under the law of the kingdom, or the royal law. This would focus attention on our inescapable obligation. Or maybe he implies that this law proceeds to us from the King Himself, because the Lord Jesus Christ (Mt. 22:39) enunciated this law as one of the two great foundation laws of the people of God. If this is the explanation, then the emphasis rests on the authority which this law should exercise over us.

Or maybe he calls it the royal law because it is the law which rules all laws, as Paul tells us in Romans 13:8ff., where he says, 'Owe no one anything, except to love one another; for he who loves his neighbour has fulfilled the law.' Paul is here saying, '*Because* you love your neighbour you will keep God's law towards him.' Love, therefore, is the enforcement, the ruling principle of all the precepts of the law of God as regards our relationship to each other. One way or the other, James is hammering home to us that there is a law which is pre-eminent, a royal law, and that royal law can be shattered in our experience if we are not obeying God's will in regard to our caring for the needy, the helpless and the lowly, if we act towards other people on any basis other than recognition of their real need, and whole-hearted concern for their true welfare.

b. The Christian is subject to the law as proceeding from God (verses 10,11)

In continuing this same theme of the Christian's obligation to the law of God, James has in mind that tendency which we all find in ourselves to pick and choose amongst the commandments of God. It is as though a person might say, 'There are two great commandments – the first, that we love the

Lord our God; the second, that we love our neighbour as ourselves – I do admit I fall down on the second, but I give all my concentration to the first.' We are all inclined to pick and choose amongst the precepts of God, and to do those things which are temperamentally suited to us.

James will not have that. He would have us recall that law is not like a heap of stones whereby we may pick some and leave others. The law is like a sheet of glass, and if it is broken it is broken. It is shattered by one breach. The law is one great whole, because it proceeds from the single Lawgiver. *He who said, 'Do not commit adultery,' said also, 'Do not kill.'* 'He who said ... said also.' Every law proceeds equally from the mind and character and will of God, and therefore every law belongs to the great unity of the divine nature.

We need to be very clear on this question of law in the life of the Christian, because it is so easy and almost automatic for us to say, in relation to a passage like this, 'But of course we are not under the law; we are under grace.' And, thank God, we are. But if we leave the matter like that, we leave it at a point of misunderstanding. Here, as in so many other ways, the Old Testament is a book of visual aids enabling us to understand the New. God brought from Egypt a people redeemed by the blood of the lamb, and the goal of their journey was Mount Sinai. God had said beforehand to Moses (Ex. 3:12): 'This shall be the sign for you, that I have sent you: when you have brought forth the people out of Egypt, you shall serve God upon this mountain.' This is equivalent to saying that Mount Sinai was the appointed immediate objective for the redeemed, and that their gathering there was the divine seal upon the work of salvation which God had wrought for them. When they came there, God gave them His law.

This, then, is the place of God's law in the life of the redeemed people. It is not a ladder by which the unsaved climbs up into salvation. The law of God is the pattern of life which God gives to a redeemed people, and He gives it to them as a reflection of His own nature so that their lives may reflect His holiness. This is true in the New Testament as in the Old (*e.g.* Lv. 19:2; 1 Pet. 1:14–16). All the principles which exist in the divine nature have been translated by God into precepts and given to His children for their obedience. We cannot pick and choose, therefore. God has given us a law.

c. The Christian is subject to the judgment of the law (verses 12,13)

The third thing James tells us really searches our hearts. The Christian is subject to the judgment of the law.

Concerning this sobering topic, James tells us three main things, and the first is this, that it is a judgment before which we are without excuse (verse 12). When we stand before the judgment seat of Christ[6] we are judged by the law of God, that is to say, by comparison with the divine nature. But, in particular, we are judged by what James calls for the second time the *law of liberty* (*cf.* 1:25). What does he mean? He means the law which, in Christ, conveys along with its commands the liberty of obedience to those who obey it.

The story is told[7] of a Japanese Christian who had been a thief before he was converted. After his conversion, on the first Sunday, he ventured into a Christian church for worship, and as he stepped inside the door he saw on the wall of the church the Ten Commandments. Out of the Commandments there leapt upon this thief the commandment, 'Thou shalt not steal.' It leapt out from the wall at him, but in a marvellously new way. It no longer said to him, 'Thou shalt *not* steal'; it said to him, 'Thou *shalt* not steal.' What had

---

[6]*Cf.* Rom. 14:10–12; 2 Cor. 5:9–11.
[7]I am indebted for this to Miss Alice Hoare whose sister, Dorothy, lived and died for the work of Christ in Japan and was involved in the incident. What is illustrated here with reference to God's commands should be linked with the basic truth of the life-giving capacity of God's Word; *cf.* 1:18,21,25.

formerly been a condemning precept was now a life-giving promise: 'thou *shalt* not steal'. So in Christ the precepts of the law have become promises to the believer, bringing the liberty of obedience. How can we stand before God and confess that we have failed, when He shall say, 'But I made it possible for you to obey?'

Secondly, we will be judged particularly, James says, on the matter of respect of persons – *judgment is without mercy to one who has shown no mercy* (verse 13). The teaching of Jesus is here re-echoed[8] and must be candidly and thoughtfully faced. An important distinction lies at the root of what both Jesus and James are saying: it is not that our mercy towards others has purchasing power but that it has evidential value. Neither James nor his Lord makes our mercy a meritorious act by which we purchase mercy for ourselves from God, but both say that without a merciful disposition towards others we can neither realistically seek nor effectively receive God's mercy for ourselves.

Take, for example, the particular mercy of forgiveness. In the model prayer, Jesus has taught us to pray 'forgive us our trespasses'. This is not, of course, to say that we can or must never plead 'forgive me', but the wording of the model prayer underlines that all true prayer is in the context of fellowship or family membership. How can I realistically pray 'forgive us' (with the implication, 'forgive X for his hurting me') unless I am at that moment myself entertaining a forgiving spirit? Can I truly ask God to forgive what I am unprepared to forgive? And if I cannot truly ask, how can I effectively receive?

James, however, is faithful to the balance of Scripture, and therefore thirdly, he concludes with a word of immense comfort that in this judgment which will search us through and through, and particularly on the point of our care for the needy, *mercy triumphs over judgment* (verse 13b). In that

[8] *E.g.* Mt. 6:14,15; 18:23–35, especially verse 35.

great day we have one eternal security: our names are written in the Lamb's book of life.[9] Mercy has embraced us, and mercy will not let us go. Here is a mysterious thing which Scripture never fully explains: the judgment seat of Christ. We shall stand there; we shall be judged there. Our eternal security will not in the least way be shaken by what happens there, but we shall be judged before Christ and He will search us, whether we have been like Him; He will search us whether we have cared mercifully for the needy. We shall be delighted with Him in that day. The question is whether He will be delighted with us.

2:14-26 The life of active consecration

14 What does it profit, my brethren, if a man says he has faith but has not works? Can his faith save him? [15]If a brother or sister is ill-clad and in lack of daily food, [16]and one of you says to them, 'Go in peace, be warmed and filled,' without giving them the things needed for the body, what does it profit? [17]So faith by itself, if it has no works, is dead.

[18]But some one will say, 'You have faith and I have works.' Show me your faith apart from your works, and I by my works will show you my faith. [19]You believe that God is one; you do well. Even the demons believe – and shudder. [20]Do you want to be shown, you foolish fellow, that faith apart from works is barren? [21]Was not Abraham our father justified by works, when he offered his son Isaac upon the altar? [22]You see that faith was active along with his works, and faith was completed by works, [23]and the scripture was fulfilled which says, 'Abraham believed God, and it was reckoned to him as righteousness'; and he was called the friend of God. [24]You see that a man is justified by works and not by faith alone. [25]And in the same way was not also Rahab the harlot justified by works when she received the messengers and sent them out another way? [26]For as the body apart from the spirit is dead, so faith apart from works is dead.

We come now to the third element in the life of faith as James portrays it to us. It is as though he were facing all over

[9]Rev. 20:15; 21:27; cf. Lk. 10:20; Jn. 10:27–29; Rom. 8:28–30; 1 Cor. 3: 11–15; Eph. 2:4ff.; Col. 1:12, etc.

again the question, But are not Christians delivered from the law? And in reply to that he asks another question, Do you really understand what faith is? Do you understand that the life of faith is the life of consecrated action, of practised obedience to whatever God may command?

The contents of these verses are easily summarized. James brings four examples of faith before us, and after each in turn he states the truths which are to be deduced from it. First there are two examples of spurious faith (verses 15, 16, 19) with the lessons drawn in verses 17, 20. Then there are two examples of genuine faith (verses 21, 25) with the lessons drawn in verses 22–24, 26. As we shall see the first and fourth examples deal with the fruitfulness of faith manward, and the second and third examples with the fruitfulness of faith Godward.

All these examples arise in answer to the question of verse 14, and we should be very careful to remark that James' meaning is misrepresented in the AV. We read there, 'Can faith save him?' and this sounds suspiciously like a challenge thrown down to the great doctrine of salvation by faith alone, as it is stated, for example, in Ephesians 2:8. It is just such misunderstandings of what James is attempting here that have led some to suppose that he gives teaching which conflicts with that of Paul.

The supposed conflict is entirely imaginary. It begins to evaporate as soon as we realize that James opens his argument by asking, 'Can *that* faith save him?' (RV, NEB) or 'Can *his* faith save him?' (RSV). That is to say, while it is undeniable that we are saved by faith alone, this doctrine is as liable to abuse as any other, and not everything that is claimed as faith is the genuine article (following the RV and NEB renderings) and not everyone who claims faith is a genuine believer (as in RSV). It is a most important exercise to discern what exactly false faith is, what genuine faith is, and to examine ourselves in the light of the result.

The first example of spurious faith is the armchair philanthropist (verses 14–17). He is a man who claims faith in God but is devoid of concern for men – even for the needs of those within the Christian fellowship, the *brother or sister*. His remedy for social ills is expressed in good advice,[1] 'Please do not worry so! All you need is some warm clothes and a meal and then you will feel ever so much better '(verse 16). But no positive action ensues. From the chosen example we learn that faith exposes its true nature, for good or ill, by its reaction to human need. If it has no practical solution, it is 'profitless' (verse 14), and 'dead' (verse 17), the general lesson being that it is not mere expression of faith which saves a man, but only that sort of faith which proves its living power by the evidence of good works (*cf.* Eph. 2:8–10).

The second example of spurious faith is the believing demons (verses 18–20). We must understand verse 18 as a connecting verse consisting of an objection and a reply. RSV makes this structure clear by using inverted commas, and NEB puts the matter beyond doubt by inserting the explanatory words 'to which I reply'. It would seem that here James is speaking to the person who objects that different Christians have different gifts, and that possibly one may be gifted in 'faith' and another more gifted in application to life. James clearly will have none of this: the only evidence of the reality of faith is that it *does* something. In particular (verse 19), he moves on to instance another side of faith's fruitfulness: it ought, by implication, to bring peace with God, but, on the contrary, the sort of 'faith' a demon professes begets nothing but trembling at the certainty of the reality of God. Consequently, it is *barren* (verse 20).

In summary, then, spurious faith is faith which is the merest expression of opinion, a bare testimony, concerning

---

[1] *Cf.* Lk. 7:50; 8:48. When the Lord said 'Go in peace', it was after the person's wants had been relieved.

which there is no visible fruit, either manward in deeds of kindness, or Godward in peace and assurance.

On the other hand, genuine faith is first exemplified in Abraham (verses 21–24).[2] The heart of James' argument here is expressed in verse 22, with the double assertion that in Abraham's case 'faith was at work in his actions' (NEB), and 'by works was faith made perfect'. Abraham is, in fact, the perfect illustration of that progress to maturity which James insisted on in 1:3,4. Faith must be challenged; if, in the face of the challenge, it is victorious, then it makes progress towards becoming a fixed characteristic of life, and moves on to genuine maturity. Abraham came to maturity when the faith he expressed in Genesis 15:6 proved victorious in the face of the challenge of Genesis 22:1f. Abraham's faith was productive Godward: productive of genuine trust in the divine promises (see Heb. 11:17–19), and productive of costly obedience in the light of which God said to him, '*Now* I know that you fear God' (Gn. 22:12). Consequently the principle of the matter is drawn out in verse 24, that *a man is justified by works and not by faith alone*, not that in any sense Abraham worked for his justification before God, or merited it by personal acts of piety, but that his works and his acts of obedience were the demonstration that the faith he professed for salvation was the genuine article.

The faith of *Rahab* (verses 25,26), which is the last example

[2]Abraham's faith is used illustratively on three main occasions in the New Testament: (1) Rom. 4; Gal. 3:6. Here it means absolute reliance on God's promises, 'however improbable their fulfilment may seem to human calculations' (Mitton); (2) Heb. 11:8, faith as obedience to a command backed by promises, involving the enduring of risks and the abandoning of securities; (3) Jas. 2:21; Heb. 11:17. Obedience to a command which seemed to contradict God's promises and which could only be obeyed at the uttermost cost. The third use embraces the first and second, for it faces Abraham again with the question of the reliability of the promises and of the extent of his personal dedication. This clarifies further that there is no conflict between James and Paul. James selects the all-inclusive example of Abraham's faith.

offered, was a faith which was fruitful manward. We are not told anything about Rahab's testimony (though it was a remarkable one; *cf.* Jos. 2:9–11). We are only told what her testimony led her to do, namely, to 'receive the messengers'. Hers was a faith concerning which there was evidence available, the evidence of out-going, sacrificial, self-forgetful concern for the welfare of others.

So much for the content and general teaching of the verses. It may help, in conclusion, to pull together the threads of the discussion by asking three questions and indicating James' answers to them.

The first question is this: What does James mean by the word 'faith' when he uses it alone? And the answer given in verses 14–20 is that he means a mere profession, the expression of an opinion concerning ourselves. All through Scripture this is discounted as useless. The Lord Jesus told a parable (Mt. 22:1–14) concerning a great king who made a wedding feast, and, when the invited guests were unwilling to come, sent out into the highways and hedges to fetch in any who could be gathered. And when he came to visit his guests he found a man who had not on a wedding garment, and he questioned him: 'Friend, how did you get in with no wedding garment?' The man was speechless, without excuse, and he was put out from the wedding feast. But who is this man? He is a man with a testimony which is not confirmed by any visible change in his life. If the king had invited testimonies at the wedding breakfast, our friend could have given an impeccable testimony. He could have said, 'On such and such a date when I was so many years old, someone came to me as I stood at the cross-roads of life and said, "Will you come and join the great king in his wedding feast?" and I said, "Yes."'

'I heard the call,
Come follow: that was all.
I rose and followed.'

57

There is nothing wrong with that testimony. But he had no wedding garment. He had none of that fine linen which is the righteous deeds of the saints (Rev. 19:8). He had a bare testimony, a testimony that did not show outwardly in his life. That is what James is against; that is what James warns us about. He warns us against leaving our standing in Christ as a matter of an expressed opinion.

Secondly, what is the teaching here about the relationship between faith and works? We need to give our attention to the question in verse 21, *Was not Abraham . . . justified by works?* and the explanatory comment in verse 22 *that faith was active along with his works, and faith was completed by works.*[3]

We have already seen in the study of the opening verses of the epistle that God's plan for our sanctification is that faith must meet and pass its tests, that tested faith becomes a fixed habit of life and when persevered with issues in full Christian maturity. We can neither escape this progression nor take short cuts in it. Faith must meet and pass its tests, and 'works' are the obedient acts of faith in the face of the promises and commandments of God and in the trials of life.

Now we have one more question. What are the primary works of faith? They are the works of Abraham and Rahab. And is it not wonderful how the Word of God brings these two together: a man and a woman, a Jew and a Gentile, a man of great sanctity in his walk with God, and a woman of great uncleanness? This shows us that these works of faith are for all the people of God, and none can make excuse.

What was the work of Abraham? It was that he held nothing back from God. God said, 'I want your son.' Abraham said, 'You can have him.' What was the work of Rahab? First of all, she saw clearly the God of Israel. She said, 'The Lord your God He is God in heaven above and on the earth

---

[3]*Cf.* E. H. Plumptre (*The General Epistle of St James*, Cambridge, 1901): 'The very form of the statement implies that the faith existed prior to the works by which it was made perfect.'

beneath' – a God in heaven, a God on earth: no other God. She gave her testimony. And then, on the basis of that testimony, she reached out, and she took into her own care and protection those who in that context were the needy, the helpless, and the outcast. She *received the messengers*.

James brings us back again, therefore, to the point which he has underscored over and over again. The life of faith is the life of imitating God in Christ Jesus. We fail in our imitation if we are not embracing the needy. The life of faith is the life of obedience, but the royal law is that we love our neighbour as ourselves, and we break it if we do not embrace the needy. The life of faith is the life of active consecration, and we cannot live that life as a private interior transaction between ourselves and God. It must be expressed outwardly in the active obedience that holds nothing back from God, and reaches out to the helpless among men.

3 WORDS AND WISDOM
3:1-18

The section of James' letter which now falls to be studied is in two unequal sections. Verse 1a matches verse 13a. The person who is wise and understanding will tend to become or to be treated as a teacher of others. But verse 1a is a warning and verse 13a an encouragement. James brings before us a dissuasive as concerning words and an exhortation to wisdom.

Two strands of thought, each typical of James, are thus woven together to form this chapter. The connection between faith and wisdom was one of the earliest items of teaching in his letter (cf. 1:2–5), and can be summarized by saying that if we are to progress from faith to full maturity then we need the wisdom from on high to be the guide of our lives. Along this line, there is a clear connection between 2:14–26 and 3:13–18. But also James has linked the new birth and the controlled tongue in a most deliberate way. Not only is control of the tongue one of the basic marks of genuine Christian experience (1:26,27) but it is singled out and somewhat set apart from the other two, suggesting that it is an issue which more than any other weighs heavily on James' heart.[1]

Along this line there is a clear connection between 2:14–26 and 3:1–12, for the controlled tongue will be a foremost mark of the outworking of true faith.

One can almost sense James weighing up in his mind which of these he should deal with first, the outworking of faith as

[1] Cf. 1:19,20; 2:12,15,16; 3:1–12; 4:11,13–15; 5:9,12.

directed by divine wisdom or as marked by the controlled tongue, for they are both basic to his understanding of the life of the Christian in this world. Why he chose to treat the tongue first we can only guess, but it may not be much wide of the mark to suggest that Christians then resembled Christians now in their over-prizing of public activities like preaching, speaking and testifying as one of the great and indeed early marks of having committed one's life to Christ. Is it not so that one of the earliest directives given to the new convert is to 'tell someone'? And can we not all recall cases where people who are no more than babes in Christ have been hastened into the public eye to pronounce on Christian subjects in a manner far beyond their experience, knowledge and wisdom? How practical is the warning, *Let not many of you become teachers* (verse 1)! To be such is to attract a closer scrutiny from God (verse 1b), and to venture into an area of activity where temptations are many and sins are easy.

It may have been thus that James, in that practical wisdom which God so plentifully gave him, was led to set before us the particular objective of the controlled tongue (verses 1–12), and then to proceed to the primary objective of the life grounded on heavenly wisdom (verses 13–18). Before we embark, however, on a study under these two headings, it is well to note that James is not calling for the silenced tongue but for the bridled tongue. He is not against preaching, teaching or testifying. He is opposed to any alacrity with which we might think that this was the greatest or the first avenue of the outworking of faith, and his wise advice is first to take the control of the tongue seriously and then to use it as a disciplined instrument to the glory of God and the enrichment of His people.

1 Let not many of you become teachers, my brethren, for you know that we who teach shall be judged with greater strictness. ²For we all make many mistakes, and if any one makes no mistakes in what he says he is a perfect man, able to bridle the whole body also. ³If we put bits into the mouths of horses that they may obey us, we guide their whole bodies. ⁴Look at the ships also; though they are so great and are driven by strong winds, they are guided by a very small rudder wherever the will of the pilot directs. ⁵So the tongue is a little member and boasts of great things. How great a forest is set ablaze by a small fire!

6 And the tongue is a fire. The tongue is an unrighteous world among our members, staining the whole body, setting on fire the cycle of nature, and set on fire by hell. ⁷For every kind of beast and bird, of reptile and sea creature, can be tamed and has been tamed by humankind, ⁸but no human being can tame the tongue – a restless evil, full of deadly poison. ⁹With it we bless the Lord and Father, and with it we curse men, who are made in the likeness of God. ¹⁰From the same mouth come blessing and cursing. My brethren, this ought not to be so. ¹¹Does a spring pour forth from the same opening fresh water and brackish? ¹²Can a fig tree, my brethren, yield olives, or a grapevine figs? No more can salt water yield fresh.

Sins of speech are not particularly remarked among Christians, at least not in a way commensurate with the importance given them in the Scriptures.² James justifies his insistence on the particular importance of the controlled tongue in a series of five reasons:

a. Because of its key place in holy living (verses 2–5a)

James opens his teaching on this note: *If any one makes no mistakes in what he says he is a perfect man, able to bridle the whole body also* (verse 2). This is more than simply saying that a controlled tongue is evidence of spiritual maturity (which is what *perfect* signifies); it is rather that the control of the tongue is the means to that maturity. The man who makes no

²*E.g.* Pss. 15:2,3; 34:13 (*cf.* 1 Pet. 3:10); 141:3; Pr. 6:16,17,19; 13:3; 18:21; Is. 3:8; 6:5; 53:9 (*cf.* 1 Pet. 2:22,23); Mt. 12:36, 37; 15:18; Eph. 4:25,29; 5:4.

mistakes in speech is *able to bridle the whole body*. Control at this one point ushers a person into a strategic position of control over all bodily passions.

This is driven home by two illustrations, the horse (verse 3) and the ship (verse 4). As to the horse, one comparatively tiny factor, the *bit*, is the means of controlling and directing the immense powers which the animal possesses. So also we are to view the tongue: this one comparatively tiny factor is the means of controlling and directing the whole body.

The point of the second illustration, the ship and its rudder (verse 4), is largely the same, but brings another aspect of the truth before us. The point is that a small factor controls a large factor, but the illustration specifies now not inherent capacities which can be thus harnessed but outside factors and assailants determining to blow us off course as Christians. It therefore calls to mind not victorious living in the matter of our own inner capacities and tendencies (the horse and the bit) but victorious living in the storms and blasts of life. Well then might the tongue 'boast of great things' (verse 5a) – and it is no hollow boast. 'It can make huge claims' (NEB), yes, and in James' view it can substantiate them: it is like the bit to the horse, controlling our unruly passions; it is like the rudder to the ship, holding course through the storm. It is the key factor in victorious, consistent living; it has a vital place in practical Christian holiness.

b. Because of its actual power for evil (verses 5b,6)

A third illustration follows at the end of verse 5: *How great a forest is set ablaze by a small fire!* The spark which starts the conflagration is again a small thing; it is infinitely smaller than the fire which results. But once that spark has taken hold, then it will spread and spread until the whole is engulfed in the flame. So the tongue possesses an actual power for evil in the life of a Christian: *The tongue is a fire . . . an unrighteous world among our members, staining the whole body, setting on fire the cycle of nature, and set on fire by hell.*

Four things are told us here about the tongue: first, its character: it is *an unrighteous world* (better, 'the unrighteous world') *among our members*. It represents, among our members, 'the world with all its wickedness' (NEB). The outside world, with its pull, with its tendency to evil, with everything that is sinful and immoral about it, has its representative right in our very nature, in our very faculties. The tongue is the representative of the world. The word 'world' is usually used in the New Testament as that which is ranged in opposition to God, for example in the sentence, 'The world knew him not' (Jn. 1:10) which we might take as a definition. The world is everything that refuses to recognize the lordship of Jesus Christ, and that world, that unruliness, that opposition to God, has its standing representative, its permanent man among our faculties. That is the character of the tongue.

Secondly, its influence: *staining the whole body*. That is to say, there is no sin that ever enters our body through the avenue of any one of our senses or faculties but the tongue is a prime mover in it, even if it is only a matter of talking to ourselves. We talk ourselves into all the sins that we commit. We argue that this is allowable, that this is timely, that this is not the opportunity to go the way of God. The tongue introduces and justifies to every one of our members in turn the sinful influence and the sinful action. In this sense it defiles the whole body.

Thirdly, we are told of its continuance: *setting on fire the cycle of nature*.[3] This is a rather uncommon and unusual ex-

[3]'The cycle of nature' was a phrase used by certain non-Christian sects to refer to recurring re-incarnations, which then passed into general use divested of its technical meaning and signifying 'little more than "the whole range of human life" or even "the ups and downs of life" ... "all the changing scenes of life"' (Mitton). Plumptre notes that, in 1:23, the similar phrase 'the face of his nature' obviously means 'natural face'. Consequently 'the wheel of nature' means ' "the natural wheel" ... the wheel which begins (at birth) to roll on its course, and continues rolling until death'.

pression; but it means something like the hymn-writer's expression 'Time, like an ever-rolling stream'. Time rolls along, and if this is James' meaning we might say that the tongue sets on fire the whole course of human life: the wheel which starts turning at birth and stops turning at death, the whole daily round, the common task, the whole course of life. As Calvin says in his commentary, 'Other vices are corrected by age or by process of time. They drop off from our lives.' Sometimes the incapacities of old age make us unable to commit the sins we enjoyed in our youth. Vices are corrected by age or by the process of time. 'The vice of the tongue', he says, 'spreads and prevails over every part of life. It is as active and potent for evil in old age as ever it was in the days of our youth.' It sets on fire the whole range of human life.

Fourthly, James speaks of its affiliation: it is *set on fire by hell*. Just as at the beginning, when he spoke of the tongue as the permanent representative of the world, he showed that it is anti-God, so now at the end of his description he says that it is pro-Satan. One is reminded very forcibly of the day of Pentecost when fire came down from heaven, and the early church was mobilized to speak a pure, intelligible, convincing word to the first hearers of the gospel so that they were able to say, 'We hear them telling in our own tongues the mighty works of God' (Acts 2:11). Fire came down to mobilize the tongue for God. So there is a fire that rises from the very pit of hell (as the word here used expresses it) to kindle within us all that Satan desires. This actual potency of the tongue to be the instrument of Satan is by no means confined to outbursts of foul language, improper stories or questionable frivolities. There was a day in his experience when Peter took the Lord Jesus Christ to one side to give Him the best advice he knew, but Jesus replied, 'Get behind me, Satan! You are a hindrance to me; for you are not on the side of God, but of men' (Mt. 16:22). The greatest and most loving exercise of human wisdom can be kindled out of the pit of hell. It is no wonder, then, that James exercises such pressure upon us to control the tongue.

c. Because of its defiance of all human restraint (verses 7,8a)

Thirdly, we are prompted to get on with this particular task of controlling the tongue by the fact of its defiance of all human restraint. In the beginning God gave man dominion (Gn. 1:28) over every other animal, and in pursuance of this they have been tamed, and they are being tamed. Man continues to exercise dominion over nature which was given to him by the Creator God. But *no human being can tame the tongue – a restless evil* (verse 8). The word 'restless' has been well translated by J. B. Phillips 'always liable to break out', like a half-tamed, untamed, or poorly tamed beast. It will accept for a moment restrictions that have been laid upon it, but then suddenly and unexpectedly it will break loose again. That is the meaning here, but the point that James is making is not just the unruliness of the tongue, not just that it is untamable and always liable to break out, but that it is untamable *by humankind.*

Twice he uses rather forcible expressions. Every other creature has been tamed 'by the native power of man' as we might translate it in verse 7, and then, taking the words in their Greek order in verse 8, the same stress is made again: 'But the tongue no-one is able to tame *of men.*' The point he is making here is that it defies human, or as we might say, merely human restriction. Neither the strength native to humanity, nor the individual power of any particular man can avail against it. Consequently, if the Christian brings his tongue into a bridle (1:26) then he has a mark upon his life which cannot be explained in terms of merely human capacity. He has a mark of the supernatural. It is tempting to imagine that James was thinking, as he wrote this, of his brother and his Lord: 'No man ever spoke like this man' (Jn. 7:46); or again, 'You have the words of eternal life' (Jn. 6:68); or again, '(They) wondered at the gracious words which proceeded out of his mouth' (Lk. 4:22).

The Lord Jesus was impressive in His tongue. There is a very remarkable thing in Isaiah 53:9. Speaking of the Servant of the Lord, foretelling the Lord Jesus Christ, Isaiah said, 'There was no deceit in his mouth.' He insists that the perfection of the Servant of God was seen specifically in His controlled tongue. We could understand why Isaiah made this emphasis, if he had had the benefit of reading James; but nobody has yet suggested that Isaiah lived after James! In making this emphasis, that the perfect man has a controlled tongue, was Isaiah not reaching back in his own experience to the day when he was himself confronted by the holiness of God, and all the sinfulness of his nature rose up into his conscience at this one point? 'Woe is me! for I am lost; for I am a man of unclean lips' (Is. 6:5). The uncleanness of the lips was, to him, the particular evidence of his fallen nature, the particular factor which unfitted him for the presence of God, and as he looked forward to the blessed, coming Servant of God, he discerned One who would show His perfection by a controlled tongue.

Surely we wish to be like Christ in this world! Surely we feel the urgency to have something about us which the world cannot explain! The tongue has not been tamed by the native power of man. But what about the powers of the new birth?

d. Because of its involvement in the deadly sin of inconsistency (verses 8b–11)

James continues in his encouragement to us to make the control of the tongue a particular objective. He speaks here of its involvement in the deadly sin of inconsistency – another of his favourite themes (1:6–8; 2:4).

There is something more here than the co-existence of blessing and cursing. That in itself would show that we are divided in our nature, that we are inconsistent, if now we bless and now we curse. The point rather is that we bless and curse the same object. In one setting we adore God, and in another setting we revile Him, as He is seen in His likeness in our fellow-men. There is our inconsistency.

James brackets this evidence of inconsistency with two pointers to the poisonous nature of the tongue. He says in verse 8 that it is *full of deadly poison*, and asks in verse 11 if a fountain can *pour forth from the same opening fresh water and brackish*. The point of the illustration is this, that if it were possible for a fountain from the same well-spring to send out both sweet water and bitter, we would never know it, because the bitter water would prevail. The damage of the sin of inconsistency in the life of the Christian is that it sours even our worship of God. If we are blessing God when we look up to Him in heaven, and cursing Him when we see His likeness in our fellow-men; if we are loving Him there and hating Him here, whether it is the sweet water of the upward prayer or the bitter water of the manward curse, the curse is prevailing. Our inconsistency sours even the best efforts of the tongue.

e. Because it is an index of the heart (verse 12)

Over and over again, then, James calls us to use all our endeavours after this particular objective, a controlled tongue, but he still has one final reason to add for his urgency, namely that the tongue is an index of the heart. *Can a fig tree, my brethren, yield olives, or a grapevine figs? No more can salt water yield fresh.* It is 'out of the abundance of the heart' that 'the mouth speaks' (Mt. 12:34).

In other words, James returns at the end to the point he made at the beginning: there is an inexplicable axis linking

69

the tongue and the inner seat of human nature, so that they move as one. On the one hand, to control the tongue is to control the whole person (verse 2), and on the other hand, what happens in our tongue is an index of what the heart is like (verse 12). The bitter fruit of words proceeds from the corrupt root of the heart.

3:13–18 The primary objective

13 Who is wise and understanding among you? By his good life let him show his works in the meekness of wisdom. 14But if you have bitter jealousy and selfish ambition in your hearts, do not boast and be false to the truth. 15This wisdom is not such as comes down from above, but is earthly, unspiritual, devilish. 16For where jealousy and selfish ambition exist, there will be disorder and every vile practice. 17But the wisdom from above is first pure, then peaceable, gentle, open to reason, full of mercy and good fruits, without uncertainty or insincerity. 18And the harvest of righteousness is sown in peace by those who make peace.

The particular Christian objective of a controlled tongue is now set in a context typical of the way in which James, and indeed the whole Bible, thinks. Important though it is, the use of the tongue is only one possible mode by which our faith is outwardly expressed in works, but if this is to happen then there is a prior requirement, the inner wisdom to guide life aright.

We have already seen in our introductory remarks on chapter 3, and by referring back to 1:2–5, how true this is to James' teaching: the outworking of the life of faith depends on God's gift of wisdom. But essentially the same truth is basic in Paul's teaching: the Christian life is not applied like make-up to the outside of our personalities, but is an outgrowth from an inner transformation. This is why, for example, Paul speaks of certain great characteristics as 'the fruit of the Spirit' (Gal. 5:22), or 'the fruit of the light' (Eph. 5:9). A great inner change has taken place; God's Spirit has

come to reside in the heart; native darkness has been transformed into 'light in the Lord'; the new centre must appear
in the new circumference. In the same way, as regards the
mode of outworking whereby the new nature becomes visible
in life, Paul teaches that we are to 'be transformed by the
renewal of your mind' (Rom. 12:2), which we understand as
a positive call to direct our minds to new topics of thought,
new imaginings, new ambitions. Correspondingly, Paul
contrasts the unconverted with the converted by speaking of
the former as futile in the minds, 'darkened in their understanding', indwelt by 'ignorance', and the latter as a person
who has 'learned Christ' and been 'taught in him, as the
truth is in Jesus', and who is to be 'renewed in the spirit of
your minds' (Eph. 4:17–24).

This is exactly what James is now teaching. The word
'works' (3:13) looks back to the particular 'work' of the
controlled Christian tongue (verses 1–12), and beyond that
to the insistence (2:14–26) that genuine faith is active in
works. Such 'works' can only proceed from a transformed
inner life, a heart and mind imbued with the divine
wisdom.

This, then, is the primary objective for every Christian,
and in verses 13–18 James reviews three aspects of it.

a. The primary importance of Christian character (verse 13)

It is possible that at this point we might try to be more practical than James – a hazardous and ill-advised task! But we
might say, 'Very well, James, you call us to show our faith
by our works; you caution us not to rush into speech; what
are we to do?' And James replies not with verbs but with
adverbs, not with directives to this or that activity but with
the requirement of a certain spirit which is to fill all activity,
whatever it may be. We might desire him to specify
conduct, whereas he insists on character: 'Let his fair and

lovely life pervade all his works with the meekness of wisdom.'[4]

What, then, is the first mark of Christian character? Almost certainly our automatic reply is 'Love', but in very many scriptures the answer is meekness. Jesus declared this in the first of the Beatitudes: 'Blessed are the poor in spirit' (Mt. 5:3). Likewise Paul urges that Christians are to exercise their gifts with lowliness of mind (Rom. 12:3), and that we are to walk worthy of the vocation to which we are called in all lowliness (Eph. 4:1f.). Over and over again the New Testament says that meekness, a proper lowly regard of ourselves, is the characteristic which is to pervade all life and all our actions. It is the opposite of arrogance, the opposite of self-importance, the opposite of self-assertiveness. It is an acceptive attitude, an attitude of non-retaliation. It stands in contrast with *jealousy and selfish ambition* (verse 14) – the jealousy which grudges what the other person has in gifts and influence, and the self-centred ambition which wants every gift for self. 'Meekness' is the attribute of Jesus, who said, 'I am meek and lowly.' The likeness of Christ! If we want to be discerning Christians, says James, then let us put the whole weight of Christian endeavour into the task of producing that Christian character which will impress the world with its loveliness.[5]

---

[4]The unity of Scripture is a satisfying study, especially in the case of James and Paul who have been so often and undiscerningly set in contrast to each other. Phil. 2:12–16 gives the same teaching as James in respect of the primary outworking of faith in terms of character. The outworking of the Philippians' God-given salvation is not specified in this good work or that, but in everything being done 'without grumbling', *etc*. When Paul does then speak of testimony (Phil. 2:16), it is something which proceeds out of the attractiveness of Christian character.

[5]*His good life* (verse 13) signifies 'his admittedly attractive life'. 'The word . . . implies that it must be obvious to others that his way of life is good' (Tasker). This is to be the first target of the 'wise and understanding', the people of moral insight and intellectual capacity.

b. The requirement of inner consistency (verse 14)

The divided man will never get anywhere with or for God (*cf.* 1:6–8; 2:4; 3:9–12), and a pretended consecration is no consecration at all. Nothing is easier than for the Christian to go the way of Ananias and Sapphira (Acts 5:1ff.), who testified to having given all, but privately kept back part. Their deadly sin lay in their pretence; it was thus that they lied to the Holy Spirit (Acts 5:3,4,9). A cloak of *meekness* (verse 13) thrown over a heart filled with *bitter*[6] *jealousy and selfish ambition*[7] is falsehood to *the truth*.

Such pretence flouts the truth in three ways. It conceals the truth about that particular person, displaying him for what in fact he is not; it evades the message of the truth for, as we saw, the Word of God is primarily directed to the heart to produce a new life which from thence will pervade the whole; and it contradicts the truth as definitively displayed in the Person of the Lord Jesus whose character and conduct, words and works were a perfectly integrated and harmonious whole. Christian holiness proceeds from within, is energized by the word which has brought the new man to birth (*cf.* 1:18), and results in Christian wholeness, the full-grown man in Christ (*cf.* Eph. 4:13–16).

c. The conflict for holiness (verses 15–18)

These four verses bring us to a topic of immense practical importance: the conflict for holiness, the battle to live a sanctified life.

Let us look for a moment at the end of verse 14: *Do not ... be false to the truth.* James is speaking to Christians, to those who know the truth, but the very words used make it clear

---

[6]The same word which, in verse 11, is translated 'brackish'. Just as the 'bitter' water sours the whole fountain, so 'jealousy' (see above on verse 13) sours the whole life.

[7]See above on verse 13. Tasker quotes Hort: 'The vice of a leader of a party created for his own pride.'

that knowledge of the truth is one thing and living according to the truth is another. The possession of the truth is no guarantee that we are going to obey it. Once more James faces us with an important fact which he has already stressed twice. He told us (1:13–18) that the possession of the birth from above does not automatically and of itself produce the life from above, for the man who is undoubtedly born of God (1:18) is the man who is still well aware of the entice-ment and pull of the tempting voice of the old nature (1:13,14). The mere presence of the new birth does not, of itself, guarantee the victory.

Likewise again (1:21) he told us that as Christians the Word of God – that potent Word – is planted in our hearts, but (as the Lord Jesus Christ so clearly taught) the Word may be neglected and snatched away, the Word may lie in shallow, rocky soil, which does not promote growth, the Word may be choked with the pleasures and cares of this world and other desires entering in. It is one thing to possess the Word, the growth of the Word is another.

The same truth again is forced upon us. We may have the truth in our hearts, and yet lie against it. James shows us this by bringing us into this arena where two different wisdoms are battling for possession of the Christian, and the Christian has to enter into the thick of that conflict and say, 'Here I stand.'

The first of two wisdoms is described in verses 15,16. He tells us of its nature (verse 15), its characteristics (verse 16a), and its results (verse 16b). As to its nature, it is *earthly*, *unspiritual*, *devilish*. It is *earthly*, that is to say it is tied and bound to this world. It is *unspiritual*; that is, it has never been touched, or influenced, or sanctified by the Spirit of God. It is devilish, or as Wesley says, 'such as Satan breathes into the soul'.

As to its characteristics (verse 16a), it is jealous and full of selfish ambition. So whenever jealousy and selfish ambi-tion (*cf.* on verse 13) arise in the heart we know which wisdom

74

we are following. James writes these things by way of identification and warning. He will identify for us the wisdom which is not from above, so as to warn us against it. It is a wisdom which is bound into this earth, which is untouched by the Spirit of God, and which Satan breathes into the soul, and its characteristics are jealousy and selfish ambition. How unlike the Lord Jesus Christ who (Phil. 2: 6–8), though He was in the form of God, did not count it a thing to be grasped at to be equal with God! Placed in that favoured position, He neither grudged the Father His primacy, nor did He reach out to grasp it for Himself, but He went the way of lowliness; He took upon Himself the form of a servant; He was born in the likeness of men. More, even, than that, being found in human form He humbled Himself; He carried His obedience even to death on the cross. How contrasting He is to these others! No jealousy or self-ambition there. If further condemnation of the wisdom-not-from-above were needed, surely it is its failure to match the truth as it is in Jesus.

Thirdly, the results of this wisdom are *disorder and every vile practice* (verse 16b). The word *disorder* previously appeared to describe the double-minded man 'unstable' in all his ways (1:8). The fruit of the wisdom that is not from above is thus James' abhorred sin of inconsistency. The additional result of *every vile practice* is added to show that inconsistency cannot be hedged in. Just as in the illustration of the spring (3:11) the brackish water prevails, so inconsistency perverts the springs of life and every sort of shoddy worthlessness is possible.

By contrast, however, there is another wisdom (verses 17,18). It is from above and it is the exact contradiction of the hell-inspired wisdom which James has just reviewed.[8]

[8]We ought not miss the significance of James' assertion that this is a Satan-inspired *wisdom*. The example of Peter (Mt. 16:22,23) again helps. A line of thought may appear to have complete cogency, a line of action represent itself as appropriate and even beneficial, yet when it is brought under judgment of the Word of God, the example of Jesus and a conscience enlightened by the Holy Spirit (*cf.* 1 Tim. 1:19) it is discredited.

He shows its origin (verse 17a), its characteristics (verse 17b), and its results (verse 18).

First, then, as to its origin (verse 17a), it is *from above*. We may relate this at once to the invitation (1:5) that 'if any . . . lacks wisdom, let him ask God'. There is a wisdom which comes from above, and it comes in answer to prayer. The battle for holiness is to this extent a battle for prayer.

Secondly, for identification purposes, we read what are the characteristics of this heavenly wisdom, so that when we see these things or have the opportunity to exercise them, we may lay hold upon that wisdom and obey it.

He tells us, first of all, that it is *pure*. It has what is of special value to God: moral purity and holiness. The first objective of the wisdom from above is to produce in us the life that pleases God.

Next, we learn what this wisdom is towards others. It is peaceable, that is, peace-loving and peace-making. The Bible has precious little room for the person who insists on speaking his mind irrespective of the consequences. The Bible values the peace-loving and peace-making man in Christian fellowship. 'Blessed are the peacemakers, for they shall be called sons of God' (Mt. 5:9). The heavenly wisdom makes peace by being *gentle* and *open to reason*. *Gentle* expresses its attitude toward others, an attitude of the utmost considerateness, not asserting its own rights but considering their rights. Furthermore, it makes peace with others by its reaction towards them, for it is described as *open to reason*, that is, it can be appealed to. The man who is governed by the wisdom from above is an approachable man: one can come to him, one can share one's doubts or problems with him, and one knows that what he says will be governed by the truth and not by his own selfishness.

Finally, we are told what this peace-loving and peace-making wisdom is in its actions toward others, that it is *full of mercy and good fruits*. First of all, it is *full of mercy*. It displays that great work of faith which was stressed in chapter 2 – care for those who are in need of mercy and pity. But it does not stop at mercy. It has every other good work for them as well.

The third aspect of the heavenly wisdom, matching what it is before God and towards others is this, what it is to the eye of self-examination. To God 'pure': to others 'peace-loving and peace-making', and to the eye of self-examination *without uncertainty or insincerity*. *Uncertainty* is again our old friend inconsistency – the same word, the same idea. To the eye of self-examination, the person who is governed by the wisdom from above is sound through and through; there is no alien disposition, no vacillating, no inconsistency. Neither is there any element of pretence, for it is without *insincerity*.

This wisdom is not ours without conflict. Since wisdom is given in answer to prayer (*cf.* 1:5), we are called to battle for a disciplined prayer life. Furthermore, we are in the arena of moral conflict, day by day, moment by moment to say 'no' to the other wisdom, to reject its marks, to root out of our lives all such filthiness, and to build and plant in our lives those things which accord with the Word of God, and the wisdom from on high.

To encourage us on in this unremitting conflict, James tells us of the results of the wisdom from above: *the harvest of righteousness* (verse 18). Righteousness has a very steady meaning in the Bible. It means what is right in the sight of God. The result, therefore, of following the heavenly wisdom is a life that is utterly pleasing to God. Oh, that we might lay hold upon this wisdom in order to produce that fruit! But notice the soil out of which that fruit grows. *The harvest of righteousness is sown in peace by those who make peace.* How important Christian fellowship is!

One of the saddest things about local churches is when they pay so little heed to quarrels among their members. Were any Christian congregations found to harbour rioting and drunkenness, chambering and wantonness, what shock and surprise would be felt! But it is not infrequent to find the uprising of strife and envy, and to think nothing of it (Rom. 13:13). And yet Christian fellowship, says James, is the soil out of which there will grow the fruit of a life that is pleasing to God.

Thus in its fruit the wisdom from on high knits together all its characteristics: it is first *pure*, pleasing to God; secondly it is *peaceable* to men; and in that context it brings forth a life that is utterly right with Him; but it demands for its growth to harvest a fellowship of harmonious believers. May we enter into the arena, into the conflict, of the wisdom that is from on high, for the fruit of Christian character in ourselves and in our churches!

4 THE BATTLE FOR HUMILITY
4:1 - 5:6

Fellowship is one of the most frequently mentioned and most frequently neglected subjects among Christians. In the formal sense, most Christian gatherings close with the words 'the fellowship of the Holy Spirit', a prayer that we may know among ourselves such a reality of mutual and understanding love as only the Spirit of God could impart. At the centre of Christian worship there is the fellowship of the Lord's table, where 'we who are many are one body, for we all partake of the one bread' (1 Cor. 10:17). But in actuality it is clear that in many, many cases the fellowship displayed and offered by the local church is neither as credible nor as attractive as that to be found elsewhere in the locality.

The importance of fellowship evangelistically cannot be overstressed. Only a unanimous and mutually loving church can stand up to and make inroads upon its spiritually hostile environment (*cf.* Phil. 1:27 – 2:4[1]). On the individual level also, fellowship is a vital consideration. The 'harvest of righteousness' in our lives, as much as in our churches, requires as its soil 'peace' maintained 'by those who make peace' (Jas. 3:18). 'Righteousness' is consequent upon peacemaking and peace-keeping. Too readily we estimate that it is the hastiness or ill-temper of the other person which is marring fellowship; too readily we expect to find peace while Scripture calls us to make it; too readily we overlook and excuse in ourselves the roots and causes of dissension.

[1]*Cf.* the comment on this passage in J. A. Motyer, *The Richness of Christ*, Studies in Philippians (London, 1966).

These are the things which James would now have us to face. Chapter 3 ends with 'peace'; chapter 4 opens with 'wars'. James undertakes to set us on our way towards that coveted 'harvest of righteousness' by exposing and calling for the eradication of the foul crop of hostility within the Christian church. But in doing so, he is quick to point out that, in his view, by tolerating and participating in breaches of fellowship, Christians practise 'friendship with the world' (verse 4), whereas the third great mark of a genuine Christian experience (1:27) was to 'keep oneself unstained from the world'. The topic which begins with chapter 4, therefore, not only arises directly out of the teaching of chapter 3 but also elaborates the third of the cardinal virtues of the Christian, the unstained life.

4:1–5 Friendship with the world exposed

1 What causes wars, and what causes fightings among you? Is it not your passions that are at war in your members? ²You desire and do not have; so you kill. And you covet and cannot obtain; so you fight and wage war. You do not have, because you do not ask. ³You ask and do not receive, because you ask wrongly, to spend it on your passions. ⁴Unfaithful creatures! Do you not know that friendship with the world is enmity with God? Therefore whoever wishes to be a friend of the world makes himself an enemy of God. ⁵Or do you suppose it is in vain that the scripture says, 'He yearns jealously over the spirit which he has made to dwell in us'?

In these opening verses, then, what James is, in effect, doing is to expose to our gaze what friendship with the world is. In order to come as quickly as possible to the heart of his teaching, we may note that the word *passions* occurs twice (verses 1,3).

The first thing to notice about the word is that it does not necessarily mean anything wrong. It simply conveys in itself the idea of self-pleasing, or personal gratification. It may be something wrong, but it need not be. For James is not here concerned to say that this or that pleasure is wrong and marks a person out as worldly. He is expressing the underlying principle, the principle of seeking gain for self and of putting self-gratification at the centre of things.[2]

a. Towards others (verses 1,2a)

In the interests, James says, of self-gratification, of getting and having for self, we are ready to go to war with others. By the phrase *passions that are at war in your members*, he has in mind not a conflict of desires and passions within ourselves,[3] but that all our desires and passions are like an armed camp within us, and at a moment's notice they are ready to go out to war against anybody who stands in the way of some particular gratification which we want for ourselves. It is that inner thing, the putting of self at the centre, the demand that self should be satisfied, which leads to wars and fightings in the Christian fellowship. Prolonged animosities (*wars*) and sudden quarrels (*fightings*) all alike spring from this single cause.

Murder exists in the Christian 'fellowship' in the sense of that continuing resentment which our Lord equated with the taking of our brother's life (Mt. 5:21). 'Any one who hates his brother is a murderer', is John's unequivocal concurrence with his Lord's teaching (1 Jn. 3:15). The physical actuality can be studied in Cain's envious hatred of Abel (Gn. 4:1ff.), David's lust for Uriah's wife (2 Sa. 11), and Ahab's murderous covetousness of Naboth's vineyard (1 Ki. 21); the spiritual equivalent is too often ignored.

---

[2]It is not inappropriate to recall here a striking statement setting out the purpose of UNESCO: 'Since wars begin in the mind of men, it is in the minds of men that the defence of peace must be constructed.'

[3]On this important aspect of the psychology of the Christian see the identical terminology of Rom. 7 : 23.

The same sad truth about Christians now appears in the setting of fellowship with God, as James introduces the subject of prayer: *You do not have, because you do not ask.* This is a tremendous assertion of the liberty of the Christian in the presence of God, and of the glorious liberality of answered prayer when we come to the God who will withhold no good thing from those who walk uprightly (Ps. 84:11) but rather, with His only Son, freely gives us all things (Rom. 8:32). But into this relationship of free request and generous giving there comes this disturbing factor: *You ask and do not receive, because you ask wrongly, to spend it on your passions.* It is the same uprising of self-centredness which was first seen to disrupt Christian fellowship and now is seen to intrude even into the place of prayer, breaking our harmony with God.[4]

Without any violence to the text, we could translate James' next words in verse 4 'such friendship . . .', that is, 'such friendship with the world' as has been described in the preceding words, this 'friendship with the world' which consists in putting self at the centre. Once more it is not this or that activity, this or that pleasure, which constitutes worldliness. The worldly person is the self-centred person. When we put self at centre we are adopting for ourselves the very essence of the world.

What happens when this worldly friendship, this desire to satisfy and gratify the self, enters into our relationship with God? First, there is the broken marriage (verse 4). *Unfaithful creatures!* is altogether too weak for an original which plainly means 'adulteresses'.[5] As Christians we are espoused to Christ as His bride, and the marriage metaphor more than

---

[4]Dr J. G. S. S. Thomson, preaching on this passage at the South of Ireland Convention in 1968, remarked, 'We must either cleanse our hearts or stop our prayers.'

[5]*Cf.* RV, but not 'adulterers and adulteresses' as AV.

any other brings out that dimension of intimate and personal oneness with Himself which the Lord graciously grants to us.[6] But when we rush off in love with the world,[7] which, in this context, means putting self at centre – whether the particular thing in which the self is to be gratified be in itself good or bad – then the marriage vow is broken and we become guilty of adultery. Our action reveals all that is sham and bogus in our love for the Lord Jesus Christ.

Secondly, there is the broken harmony, for *friendship with the world is enmity with God* (verse 4). Peace with God is the very firstfruits of Calvary (Jn. 20:19,20). The greatness of the work of Christ upon the cross is just this that 'while we were enemies we were reconciled to God by the death of his Son' (Rom. 5:10); He has made 'peace by the blood of his cross' (Col. 1:20). But when self-centredness, the insistence on self-gratification, enters in, peace flies out and enmity replaces it. Therefore we may say that every last trace of worldliness in us indicates to what extent we have failed to appreciate the saving work of Christ and the meaning of the cross.

Thirdly, when self-pleasing invades our relationship with God, there is the broken heart (verse 5). James lays considerable stress on this aspect by calling to his aid the testimony of Scripture, as though by this means to silence any who might be disposed to reply to his previous strictures.[8] The matter, however, which he elicits from the Scriptures is expressed in words which are capable of differing interpre-

---

[6]*Cf.* Rom. 7:1–6; 2 Cor. 11:2; Rev. 19:7.9; also Je. 2:1–3; Ho. 2:14–20, *etc.*
[7]*Cf.* 2 Tim. 4:8,10; note the alternative objects of love.
[8]What scripture is James quoting when he uses the words *the scripture says*? H. Alford (*The Greek Testament*, Cambridge, 1874) urges that 'there is nothing improbable in the idea that James may have combined the general sense of Scripture on the point of God's jealousy over his people'. In Dt. 32:10,19 (LXX) he finds 'the elements of the sense of that which is cited'.

tations,[9] and it is by no means easy to decide what in particular James may have meant, for more than one line of meaning suits the context. Since, however, the emphasis rests without doubt on the idea of the divine jealousy,[1] the balance of probability is in favour of the translation offered by RSV.

A similar line of thought expressed by Paul in Romans 8:10–16 may help us to grasp what James is teaching. Paul there says that 'your spirits are alive because of righteousness' (verse 10): the position of the justified sinner is that because of this new relationship to God he has been brought to life, and the evidence of this life is seen when, prompted by the Holy Spirit, the quickened spirit of man cries out 'Abba! Father!' (verses 15, 16). James, basing his whole teaching as we saw on the fact of the new birth (1:18), starts from the fact of this inward renewal, and he depicts God as longing with a pure and jealous passion for the undistracted love of our spirits for Him. When, however, He sees us filled with an alien affection, loving and pleasing ourselves rather than Him, He knows the agony of unrequited love. 'He yearns jealously' – a verb expressive of homesick longing. What a

[9]Mitton summarizes the possibilities with impressive skill. 1. 'The spirit is either (a) subject: 'the spirit yearns', or (b) object: '(God) yearns over the spirit'. 2. 'The spirit' is either (a) the Holy Spirit, given by God to indwell His people, or (b) the spirit which God breathed into man (Gn. 2:7). 3. 'Jealously' is in the Greek a noun, 'jealousy', and it signifies either (a) God's longing for the full devotion of His 'bride', or (b) the evil quality which infects the human heart. All the major versions end as some possible combination of these alternatives.

[1]In our experience, jealousy is so often a rather repellent manifestation of possessiveness, verging on a pathological insistence on self-centredness, that doubt is sometimes entertained whether it could be an emotion consistent with the true righteousness of God. Jealousy, however, properly considered is an essential ingredient of true love: it is, on the one hand, an unceasing longing for the loved one's true welfare, and on the other hand a pure desire for a responsive love as intense and undistracted as the love which has been extended. In these great senses, the Bible insists on the jealousy of God over and for His people. Cf. Ex. 20:5; 34:14; Dt. 4:24; 5:9; 6:15; Ezk. 39:25; Joel 2:18; Zc. 1:14; 8:2, etc.

remarkable thought: that God envies the sinful self which we so thoughtlessly put at the centre of things and devote ourselves to it! He envies it, for He sees us loving it more than Him.

In these three aspects of the effect of 'friendship with the world' – the broken marriage, the broken harmony, and the broken heart – there is a distinct progression, a greater and yet greater failure on our part to respond to the love of God. The first reveals how superficial is our love for Him; the second, how little we appreciate His saving work; and the third, deepest wound of all, how we fail to respond to that intensity of divine love which sent forth the Son to redeem us, and having thus made us sons, sent the Spirit of the Son into our hearts crying 'Abba! Father!' (Gal. 4: 4ff.).

4:6 – 5:6 The blemishes of the world removed

6 But he gives more grace; therefore it says, 'God opposes the proud, but gives grace to the humble.' [7]Submit yourselves therefore to God. Resist the devil and he will flee from you. [8]Draw near to God and he will draw near to you. Cleanse your hands, you sinners, and purify your hearts, you men of double mind. [9]Be wretched and mourn and weep. Let your laughter be turned to mourning and your joy to dejection. [10]Humble yourselves before the Lord and he will exalt you.

11 Do not speak evil against one another, brethren. He that speaks evil against a brother or judges his brother, speaks evil against the law and judges the law. But if you judge the law, you are not a doer of the law but a judge. [12]There is one lawgiver and judge, he who is able to save and to destroy. But who are you that you judge your neighbour?

13 Come now, you who say, 'Today or tomorrow we will go into such and such a town and spend a year there and trade and get gain'; [14]whereas you do not know about tomorrow. What is your life? For you are a mist that appears for a little time and then vanishes. [15]Instead you ought to say, 'If the Lord wills, we shall live and we shall do this or that.' [16]As it is, you boast in your arrogance. All such boasting is evil. [17]Whoever knows what is right to do and fails to do it, for him it is sin.

1 Come now, you rich, weep and howl for the miseries that are coming upon you. [2]Your riches have rotted and your garments

are moth-eaten. ³Your gold and silver have rusted, and their rust will be evidence against you and will eat your flesh like fire. You have laid up treasure for the last days. ⁴Behold, the wages of the labourers who mowed your fields, which you kept back by fraud, cry out; and the cries of the harvesters have reached the ears of the Lord of hosts. ⁵You have lived on the earth in luxury and in pleasure; you have fattened your hearts in a day of slaughter. ⁶You have condemned, you have killed the righteous man; he does not resist you.

Reviewing 4:1–5, there are four things plainly involved in this friendship with the world. Taking them as they arise in the verses, there is, first, a wrong understanding of ourselves (verse 1), as though we and our gratifications were the centre of the universe; secondly, there is a wrong attitude towards things (verse 2), for in the pursuit of self-gratification we are shown as drawn on by covetousness; thirdly (verse 2), there is a broken fellowship with other people, whom we see as entirely dispensable in order that we may get our own way; and fourthly, there is the broken union with God (verses 2a–5).

James now turns (4:6 – 5:6) to take each of these things (but in a different order) and to call for their removal from our lives. Firstly, he shows us how we are to walk harmoniously with God (verses 6–10), urging that this is in fact the only way to complete self-fulfilment, with an implied contrast with the self-seeking attitude condemned in the previous verses. Secondly, he calls for a new relationship of humility towards others (verses 11,12), manifested in the repudiation of arrogant, critical talk. Thirdly, he brings us to a new mind concerning ourselves, by exposing the presumptuousness which so often marks our lives and pointing us to a better way (verses 13–17). And, fourthly, he charges us to beware of covetousness of wealth (5:1–6).

It is interesting to note that this new order is very nearly a reversal of that in 4:1–5. There James was diagnosing, but here he is prescribing. In diagnosing, the worldly spirit is most easily seen in our attitudes towards possessions and towards ourselves, and then it works deeper, affecting our relationships with others and with God. But the remedy must necessarily start at the root of the malady. Therefore James calls on us first to get right with God, and then to chase the symptoms of worldliness one by one right out of our lives.

There is one other general observation to be made before we look at the details of the verses. The passage is filled with commands and obligations: *Submit* (4:7) .... *Draw near* .... *Cleanse* (verse 8) .... *Do not speak* (verse 11) .... *you ought to say* (verse 15), and so forth. What is this but to say that the blemishes of the world can only be removed from us by a stern and unremitting effort, nothing short of a battle? James has no recipe for instant sanctification. He knows no easy way to victory for the Christian. From the start he warned us that we are still in the world (1:1), subject to endless pressures (1:2), but he called us to rejoice because under these pressures and by resisting them we were walking the God-appointed pathway to maturity (1:3, 4). Here is the battle, and here is the path. He will not allow us to evade the conflict and cast away the crown. Victory is not ours for the taking, but ours for the winning.

The order of teaching in the passage, then, is this, that James first shows us what constitutes the friendship of the world (4:1–5), and then he takes the blemishes one by one (4:6 – 5:6), asking, 'Do you want pure religion and undefiled before God and the Father? Do you want to keep yourself unspotted from the world? Will you then remove the blemishes out of your life?' But as he commands us to battle, look at the glorious ways in which he starts: *But he gives more grace* (verse 6a). This is one of the most comforting verses in Scripture. It tells us that whatever we forfeit when we put self in the place of God, we cannot forfeit our salvation: 'He gives more grace.' No matter what we do to Him, God is still not beaten. Our salvation depends not upon ourselves and is not in an ultimate sense threatened by our self-centredness, because He gives more grace. Even when we break the heart of God, His response is this, to give more grace. Consequently, the removing of spots and blemishes of the world is not an exercise in mere self-reformation. There is a proffered grace for us to receive, and not only so, for He gives 'more' grace. That is, even if we were to turn to God and say, 'The supply I have had so far is not enough to carry me through in this process of cleaning up my life until it is pleasing to You', God would reply, 'Well, you may have more.' His resources are never at an end. His patience is never exhausted. His initiative never stops. 'He gives more grace.'

a. Pride before God (verses 6b–10)

First of all, then, we are called to the removal of pride before God. These verses are linked to what precedes by the word 'therefore'. We have already noticed how insistently practical James is. It is not enough for him to tell us about the proffered abundance of grace (verse 6a); he must also tell us how to obtain it: it is God's gift to the humble. If we abandon proud self-exaltation, then God will give us grace. Now the same truth, but in reverse, comes again in verse 10: if we humble ourselves before God, this is in fact the true way of self-exaltation, or, as we might perhaps better say, self-fulfilment. In this way, verses 6 and 10 are like brackets, and by means of detailed commands in the intervening verses, James once more undertakes the task of practical helpfulness, showing us the details of a humble walk with God. It has four aspects.

The first requirement is active allegiance (verse 7). Two things are brought together here, and ought never to be separated: *Submit . . . to God . . . resist the devil.* How often is submission to God understood as a sort of Christian passivity! Indeed it is not unknown to preachers to call upon believers to 'yield' to God, clearly implying by that some abandonment of effort, a deliberate 'slumping down' (if the word is not too rude) in a total spiritual relaxation. This is frequently summed up as advice to the Christian in the words, 'Let go, and let God.' This sort of 'surrender', 'submission', 'yielding' – call it what you will – would make us nothing better than prisoners of war, henceforth waiting inertly for daily rations – not soldiers! James knows nothing of a submission to God that is not at the same time a resistance to the devil. His call is for active allegiance: complete submission to His commands in the cause of active service on campaign.

The second requirement is a deliberately cultivated fellowship (verse 8). It is expressed first as command, *Draw near to God*, and secondly as promise, *and he will draw near to you*. We need to beware of the tendency in ourselves to reverse this order. We often think to ourselves how easy it would be to keep a daily time with God if only we had a more vivid sense of His presence. In other words we want the promise to come before the command. Part of the conflict to which James calls us is this central battle for regularity and discipline in Bible study, prayer, private and public worship, attendance at the Lord's table, and all the other ways in which we may, by His gracious appointment, draw nigh to Him. Such fellowship does not grow without deliberate cultivation.

The third element in the humble walk with God is a thoroughgoing purification (verse 8b). It is a purification which touches the hand and the heart. It touches the outer life and the inner life. It touches deeds and thoughts, the hand being active and the heart being the thoughtful element in life. It is a purification which touches the specific act of wrongdoing, for the designation *sinners* emphasizes individual sinful acts, and the inner attitude of disloyalty in the mind. The same word *men of double mind* occurred in 1:8, and the thought many times. It is one of James' major emphases, the sin of wavering inconsistency, the sin of being two-faced with God.

In this thoroughgoing purification of our lives, notice who is to be the agent: *Cleanse your hands, you sinners*. This is not the work of the Holy Spirit; it is the work of the energized believer. Just as James said to us in 1:21 that we are to go like a gardener and hoe out the weeds from our lives and plant in the word of God, so here also it is our work to purge our behaviour and our heart.

The fourth element in a humble walk with God is unfeigned repentance (verse 9). The immediate and correct reply to this is that it is quite impossible for us to do it. Repentance is the gift of God.[2] Quite so, but 'he gives more grace'. In point of fact, every command in these verses is quite impossible for us. Grace alone makes it possible for us to walk with God just as grace alone made us the children of God to begin with. "'Tis grace that brought me safe thus far, and grace will lead me home.'[3] Just as Paul instructs us in the terms of the Christian life, by saying, 'If by the Spirit you put to death the deeds of the body' (Rom. 8:13) – calling us to the task of executioner, enabled thereto by the Holy Spirit – so James, by requiring repentance of us, reminds us that we are perpetual suppliants to God for the grace by which alone we will be able to go the way of His commandments, resist the devil, frequent God's presence, purge our hands and hearts, and live near the cross in unfeigned repentance for sin.

b. Defamation of others (verses 11,12)

The second blemish of the world on the life of the Christian is defamation. It touches our relationship and attitude

[2]*Cf*. Acts 11:18; 2 Tim. 2:25.
[3]From John Newton's hymn 'Amazing grace', *Hymns of Faith* (London, 1964), no. 50.

towards other people. *Do not speak evil*; do not defame; do not bring somebody else's character down by the way you talk about them. This is not the same as a prohibition of telling lies about someone (*cf.* Eph. 4:25), for the defamation may be perfectly true. Even so, we are not to say it. The fact that it is true gives us no permission to speak. We are not so to use our tongues as to devalue another person's character. The very word James uses, translated as *speak*, has the idea of 'talking down'. It is as if he were to say, 'Do not think that you are such a superior person, that you can afford to talk from a great height about somebody else.' There is the sin of self-exaltation in it. Therefore he underlines the sin of the tongue in destroying other people's characters.

How are we to deal with this tendency to criticize other people in a defamatory way and to exalt ourselves over them? James gives us four pointers. First of all he tells us how we are to regard each other (verse 11). We are brothers – that is, we are to look upon each other as joint, co-equal heirs of salvation. This brings us all together on the same level. We were dead in trespasses and sins; the same precious blood saved us, in spite of our demerits, against what we deserve. How dare we defame or in any other way hurt or be harsh to a brother for whom Christ died?[4]

We are not only brothers but (verse 12) we are neighbours. My fellow-Christian is not the object of criticism and defamation; he is my neighbour; he is the object of pastoral care and ministry. Supposing I do know something to his discredit, my task is not to publicize it, but to go down where he is and lift him up. I must be the Samaritan to him. He is my neighbour. Defamation begins and lives in the mind. It is something we say to ourselves about the other person long before we pass it on. But if our minds were constantly exercised in biblical attitudes, then love for our brethren in Christ would begin to rid us of censoriousness,

[4]*Cf.* Rom. 14:3, 13–15; 1 Cor. 8:10–12.

and concern for our neighbours in Christ would begin to replace hurtful defamation by helpful and caring pastoral concern.

Secondly, he shows us how we are to regard the law. A threefold wrong attitude to the law of God is detailed in verse 11. The law referred to is the royal law of 2:8, that we are to love our neighbours as ourselves. And here is a person who, far from loving his Christian neighbour and brother as himself, is defaming him in speech. In this situation James brings the notion of the law. He who speaks against his brother speaks against the law: that is to say, he looks upon the law as a precept and breaks it. Secondly, he judges the law. He looks upon the law as enshrining certain values but he thinks his right of free speech is of greater value; and therefore he devalues the law; he rejects it as a standard or value. Thirdly, he is not a doer of the law but a judge: that is to say, he is a rebel against the law as an authority. So whether as precept, as value, or as authority, he is setting himself up against the law as soon as he begins to speak evil against his brother.

Thirdly, James warns us against defamation by telling us how we are to think about God. *There is one lawgiver and judge* (verse 12). Quickly he passes from the law to the Lawgiver, because in the Bible there is no difference. The law is the outshining toward the people of God of the very content of the divine nature. The things that exist in God as principles of life have been expressed upon earth as precepts for believers. The law reflects the nature of God. Therefore James swings the light from the law that we are devaluing upon earth to the Lawgiver as He sits in heaven.

The practical bearing of James' demand that we assess our attitude towards others in the light of what God is can be expressed by saying that a life wrongly related to our fellows exposes a life wrongly related to God. To put it in another way, verses 6b–10 are fundamental to the whole matter of expunging the blemishes of the world from our lives. If we were truly and insistently walking humbly with God, then we could not fly proudly in the face of His law and defame our brother. But if we do thus defame him, the failure is in the heavenly relationship before it has appeared in the earthly.

Furthermore, it is a thing for serious and sober reflection that *there is one lawgiver and judge*, for it is none other than *he who is able to save and to destroy* (verse 12). His position as Judge is not an LLD conferred *honoris causa*; it is the effective and inescapable 'wrath of a sin-hating God', and while Toplady was gloriously correct in continuing that this wrath 'with me can have nothing to do', because 'my Saviour's obedience and blood hide all my transgressions from view',[5] yet this does not nullify the truth and dread of the judgment seat of Christ, nor absolve the Christian from making his calling and election sure.

Fourthly, as he warns us against defamation he would turn us from it by telling us how we are to think about ourselves. He rounds on us with a good deal of warmth. *But who are you that you judge your neighbour?* 'Whoever do you think you are?' Well, who do I think I am in the light of verses 7–9? A person who recognizes his sin and abject unworthiness and sinfulness before God. And I from that position of recognizing that there is nothing worthy in me, turn round to criticize somebody else! Who are we indeed to judge one another?

c. Presumptuousness towards ourselves (verses 13–17)

How different is James' idea of the world from what we commonly think! To the blemishes of pride and defamation, he now adds a third worldliness which he would have us banish from our lives: the blemish of presumptuousness which comes from a wrong understanding of ourselves.

[5] Augustus Toplady's hymn, 'A debtor to mercy alone', *Christian Praise* (London, 1957), no. 230.

What is this presumptuousness of which he speaks (verse 13)? It touches, first, life: *today . . . tomorrow . . . a year*. It is the presumption that we can continue alive at will. It touches, secondly, choice: *today or tomorrow we will go . . . and spend a year and trade*. It is presumption that we are masters of our own life so that we can decide, and lo and behold, so it will happen. It touches, thirdly, the sphere of ability: *and trade and get gain*. Of course it will succeed! It is the presumption of our own ability.

One of the functions that Scripture fulfils towards us is that it teaches us the real nature of sin. Verse 13 is very far from being the commonly accepted picture of an arrogant person. For one thing, it is all so ordinary. That is exactly the point. When James exposes the blemish of presumptuousness, he exposes something which is the unrecognized claim of our hearts from time to time. We speak as if life were our right. We speak as if our choice were the deciding factor. We speak as though we had the ability to make ourselves succeed: the presumption that my life belongs to me! That is what James is against.

Now how do we guard against presumptuousness? Notice the three verbs in verses 14, 15: *you do not know, you are, you ought*. The three things here stated about us will put us on our guard against presumptuousness. First, our ignorance: *you do not know*. Observe the irony. Here is the man in verse 13 who lays out before us his programme for a year ahead, and James replies, 'But you do not know what is going to happen tomorrow!' It is not within our power to see two minutes ahead, let alone two days or two years. Let us recognize our ignorance lest we be like the rich fool who said, 'I have ample goods laid up for many years.' But God said to him, 'But this night your soul is required of you' (Lk. 12:16–21).

Secondly, our frailty. *You are a mist that appears for a little time and then vanishes*. We are insubstantial, a vapour, something that cannot stand up to the least puff of alien wind. Our life is brief: we appear for a little time. Our life is transient, and then it vanishes away as though it had never been. Its earthly existence is utterly, utterly at an end. Such is our life in its frailty.[6]

Thirdly, our dependence: *You ought to say, 'If the Lord wills . . .'* (verse 15). Clearly it is not James' intention to try to banish all planning from our lives. In fact by the words *you ought to say* he actually envisages Christians looking forward, and in the light of the foregoing example of proud planning we cannot forbid him to mean that we are at liberty to plan and humbly and tentatively make decisions affecting future years as well as future days. He can hardly be thought to want us to have that morbid attitude towards the will of God which forbids any attempt to know His will prior to the date in question. But he would have us empty our lives of proud planning which does not fear and bow to the will of God and submit all things to His ordering hand. Therefore he says *you ought to say, 'If the Lord wills'*, recognizing our dependence on Him.[7] We are dependent on Him for life, *'If the Lord wills, we shall live,'* and for activity, *'and we shall do this or that'* (verse 15).

In verse 14 it was the contents of tomorrow which were unknown, but in verse 15 it is the very existence of tomorrow and our existence that is in question. We may take tomorrow

---

[6]*Cf.* Jb. 7:7,9; Pss. 102:11; 103:15; Is. 40:6,7.

[7]The words 'God willing', or their equivalents, are not to become a fetish to us, a talisman which we carry protectively! The words should not be used unless they truly express the dependence of our hearts on Him; and if our hearts are resting in His will, the words may be used but need not always or slavishly be repeated. Calvin notes that 'we read everywhere in the Scriptures that the holy servants of God spoke unconditionally of future things, when yet they had it as a principle fixed in their minds that they could do nothing without the permission of God'. Mitton contrasts 'evil doers' who make the known transience of life 'an excuse for snatching all the pleasure out of it while there is time', while 'others use it as an excuse for doing nothing', but 'James refers to it as a reason why men should be humble before God'. It is pertinent to note Acts 18:21; 1 Cor. 4:19; 16:7; Phil. 2:19,24; Heb. 6:3.

for granted, thinking of it as a space on the rim of the wheel of time, coming on inevitably as the circling years proceed, but in the Bible the years do not circle. They go in a straight line from eternity to eternity, and on that line we receive another day only by the covenanted mercies of God.[8] The very existence of tomorrow is part of our dependence on Him as is also our own life[9] and ability.[1]

How serious, then, is presumptuousness? First of all he tells us that it is utterly unacceptable to God: he calls it *arrogance* and *boasting*, a word which appears in 1 John 2:16 as 'the pride of life', and describes it as *evil* (verse 16). That is to say, when even in this little, secret and unrecognized way we forget how frail we are, and forget to depend upon Him, it is an element of the proud, boasting, human spirit that vaunts its independence. As such it is evil, utterly unacceptable to God. James does not qualify the word; he just says *evil*. It is the same word which Scripture uses about the devil, 'the evil one' and the works of the devil. It belongs to that very spirit which possesses at its centre proud independence of God. Genesis 3 reveals that this is the sin of Eden, the determination of man to be master of his own destiny, steer his own life and rest upon his own ability to be his saviour. It is *evil*.

Secondly, presumptuousness is a cardinal sin of omission (verse 17). The relationship between verses 16 and 17 is this: the particular example in the former verse is brought within the orbit of a searching general principle. This is quite clear in the Greek, which contains a connecting particle which RSV fails to bring out. It is often translated as 'therefore'[2] but admits a variety of shades of meaning. A useful paraphrase in the present instance would be: 'How true then is the

---

[8]Gn. 8:22; Je. 33:25.
[9]Ps. 104:29,30; Dn. 5:23b.
[1]Dt. 8:18; Pr. 10:22; Je. 10:23,24; Ho. 2:8,9.
[2]*Cf.* RV, NEB, excellently, 'Well then'.

maxim that . . .'[3] But what a maxim it is which the 'simple' sin of presumptousness violates! The whole idea of sinning by default has never been better or more searchingly expressed. It is a principle which, in self-examination, finds the error in even our best and finest accomplishments. It makes us cry out, even when God has granted us the greatest success in His service, that we are unprofitable servants. 'It is', says Mitton, 'a standard of perfection which convicts our best endeavours of sin. We may be able to avoid committing forbidden evil; but who can ever seize positively every opportunity of doing good?' James is not using a sledge-hammer to crack a nut. He is showing that what we might consider an insubstantial and passing feature of life, forgetfulness of our utter dependence, he sees as the hard core of that vaunting pride which is the mark and curse of fallen man.

d. Covetousness of things (5: 1–6)

Fourthly, James underscores for us the blemish of covetousness. This is one of the outstanding manifestations of selfishness, the desire to possess. When we notice (verse 1) that James addresses himself specifically to the *rich*, it is all too easy for us to feel that his words have no application to those of us who would not be regarded as amongst the world's wealthy. But this position cannot be sustained. Certainly he addresses the rich, and his words have most application to those who run the greatest risk of the temptation, but as we follow out his arguments it is plain that the covetous attitude in all its manifestations has nothing really to do with the quantity of our possessions and that his strictures come to all alike. He is talking about the sin of covetousness, which we all have to face, and which we are all called to banish.

In these six verses, he exposes four aspects of coveting

[3] *Cf.* J. B. Phillips: 'Well, remember that . . .'.

97

and he shows us the wrong that lies at the heart of each of them.

First, he shows how covetousness can appear in terms of hoarding (verses 1–3). Various sorts of wealth are here itemized: *rotted* (verse 2) suggests stored up food; *garments*, *gold* and *silver* are also mentioned.[4] When James says, *Your gold and silver are rusted* (verse 3) we see that his mind is moving in terms of metaphor, for these precious metals are not subject to rust in the ordinary way. The point is that such resources as food, clothing, gold and silver can be left lying fallow, not put to any useful purpose, simply hoarded. James is quite clear as to the outcome of such hoarding: 'The rust which has corroded the possessions will also bring about the downfall of the possessors' (Tasker).

But why is this? What is the inner fault of wealth lying fallow? The fault is that such people have *laid up treasure for* (better 'in') *the last days* (verse 3). The *last days* are the days of the imminent return of the Lord Jesus Christ. It is a comprehensive expression covering the whole time-span between the ascension and the second coming, and focuses attention on the fact that Christians should ever be looking upward in expectancy of their Lord. If Christians hoard, where is their sense of expectation? Is the Lord Jesus to come back and find that we have hoarded and hidden our resources instead of putting them to earn interest in the work of His kingdom (see Mt. 25:25; Lk. 19:20)? This, then, is one attitude towards wealth and the fault hidden at its heart.

There was a notice recently in a daily paper, advertising a block of flats. The reason given for the sale was 'Owner going away'. He could not take his block of flats with him, and so he wanted to transform them into the sort of wealth that could go with him to another place. James is not teach-

---

[4] To rely on possessions is to rely on what is intrinsically perishable (verse 2), deceitful (verse 3, the evaporating value of money), and condemnatory (verse 3b).

ing us to be improvident; he has just said to us (4:15), 'Plan years ahead if you want to, provided only that you do so according to the will of God.' But he is saying, 'Remember you live in the last days; do not let your attitude towards wealth militate against your Christian expectancy of a returning Lord.'

Secondly, he tells us that covetousness can appear as dishonesty (verse 4). Covetousness takes the form of dishonesty when we are so delighted to possess wealth for ourselves that we forget to pay our honest obligations. And the concealed fault in it, in this case, is that the cry of it goes up into the ears of the *Lord of hosts*. It is not very certain why James suddenly refers to God as *the Lord of hosts*,[5] but it may be that this is the reason: the words *of hosts* mean in fact that the Lord is He who possesses every imaginable wealth, resource and potency. How did and how does God use this immense wealth? The reply of the Bible is that He poured it out for our benefit in such a way that finally He did not even spare His only Son but freely gave Him up on our behalf. Even then He did not stop, for with that only Son He plans also freely to give us all things (Rom. 8:32). This suggestion would give great point, in this context, to the use of the title. Out of the wealth of His resources, God has paid debts which were no concern of His, debts with which for all eternity He could never be justly charged: our debt of sin. How can we, then, if we are His children, keep back, through sheer meanness, the debts which are honourably ours? And if we do so, is it not in conflict with our claim to be His children? Dishonesty in payment is discordant with a claim to be in fellowship with such a generous God.

[5]Other suggestions are that the form of the title recalls vividly the Old Testament revelation of God, a God to whom such failure to discharge honourable obligations would be utterly abhorrent. *Cf.* Lv. 19:13; Dt. 24:14; Pr. 3:27,28; Mal. 3:5. Alford quotes the opinion of Bede: 'He entitles him "Lord of hosts" in order to strike terror into those who think that the poor have no protector.'

Thirdly, James exposes covetousness showing itself as self-indulgence (verse 5). Here is the man who values wealth for the benefits and luxuries it brings to him. It does not mean that he is spending his money on gross delights, but just that he is allowing his resources to boomerang in self-indulgence. James' exposure of such a person is vivid in the extreme: it is as if he were to say, 'Oh, to be a thin beast the day the butcher comes!' Such a beast is safe. The slaughterman has no wish to count ribs! What can the *day of slaughter* be but the day of the judgment seat of Christ? If we have over-indulged ourselves, showering such resources as we possess upon our own comforts, may we not imperil our welcome before Him who 'for your sake . . . became poor' (2 Cor. 8:9)?[6] In this sense, how truly we live in a day of slaughter!

Now finally, he gives us a fourth revelation of covetousness and its faults. Covetousness is divided loyalty. James is never far from this sin of being two-faced. *You have condemned, you have killed the righteous man; he does not resist you* (verse 6).[7] Surely James, here, is having a sober reflection concerning Judas Iscariot. Judas kept the bag, and he stole what was put in it (Jn. 12:6). It was Judas who said, ' "Why was this ointment not sold for three hundred denarii, and given to the poor?" . . . not that he cared for the poor' but because he wanted the money (Jn. 12:5,6). Even when he betrayed the Lord Jesus Christ he insisted on a price (Mt. 26:14–16). Poor Judas, therefore, is the standing example of the fact that we cannot serve God and mammon. Covetousness involves divided loyalty. And when Judas went about things

[6]*Cf.* the words *on the earth* (verse 5) with the words, clearly bearing the same significance, 'in your lifetime' (Lk. 16:25). The parable provides a searching comment on James' illustrative exposure of this form of covetousness.

[7]Some take this simply as an insistence of that carelessness for human rights which sometimes marks the wealthy. *Cf.* Am. 2:6; 5:12. But the affirmative *he does not resist* is against this. We should expect rather 'he cannot . . .', and the interpretation really would require it.

like that, *the righteous man*, Jesus, put up no resistance. It was as though He said to Judas, 'You must choose between Me and money, and if you choose money, I will bow before it.' Covetousness is the sin divided loyalty, with the added warning that if we choose covetousness we depart from Jesus and He does not resist.

These are the blemishes of the world upon the lives of believers. The blemish of pride before God; of arrogant defamation of our fellow-believers; the blemish of proud, self-assured presumptuousness; the blemish of delight in what self possesses. Self-centredness is friendship with the world.

5 UNTIL THE COMING OF THE LORD
5:7 - 20

Having come thus far with James' letter, the main lines of his teaching are clear. His starting-point can be none other than the simplicity of the way of salvation. It is impossible to account for the contents of his letter and the particular ways in which he expresses himself unless behind it all there lies a salvation which is entirely of God, cannot be acquired by human merit or endeavour, and comes home to the individual by a bare reliance upon Jesus Christ. It is an entire misrepresentation of James to speak of him as an (or the) advocate of 'works'. Like Paul (*e.g.* Phil. 2:12) he is the advocate of outworking. He is not the moralist driving us with the whip of 'Do your best' and the goad of 'More, more', but the preacher of the free grace of God, which shows how free it is in that people might mistake it as an excuse for spiritual laxity, and which shows how truly divine it is in that it has power to transform the lives of those who genuinely receive it.[1]

[1] See further Introduction, pp. 12ff. and *cf.* the questions prompted by Paul's gospel, Rom. 3:7,8; 6:1. With reference to these, H. C. G. Moule, *The Epistle to the Romans* (London, 1903), pp. 156ff., asks what gospel message could give rise to the supposition that our moral conduct is of no significance. We learn, he says, 'how explicit and unreserved his delivery of the message had been, and how Justification by Faith, by faith only, meant what was said, when it was said by him. . . . St Paul must have meant by faith what faith ought to mean, simple trust. And he must have meant by justification without works, what those words ought to mean, acceptance irrespective of our recommendatory conduct.' James and Paul thus coincide, the only distinction being that Paul preaches this gospel of free, unmerited salvation from the starting-point of justification, while James starts from regeneration (1:18).

Arising from this, James has throughout insisted on the necessity of practical, visible evidence of our status as children of God. How well he would agree with Peter's call to us to 'be the more zealous to confirm your call and election' (2 Pet. 1:10)! It is not that either he or Peter (or Paul) entertains doubts about the eternal security of the elect, or allows the possibility of a fall from grace, but that they all alike call us to make absolutely certain that we are in fact Christians, and to rest this claim on the unassailable evidence of a transformed life.

The particular form of this life is determined by the way in which God has made us His own. James begins with the new birth (1:18). In this way, both by the terms of the metaphor itself and by his exposition of it, he shows that salvation is all of God. Just as in human experience, however, birth is not an end in itself but looks forward to life, and just as parental characteristics tend to reappear in the developing child, so also with the new birth: God's choice of the helpless and needy to become His children, His speaking of the life-giving Word and His objective of 'firstfruits' predetermine the sort of life that will follow, a life of mercy, pure speech and holiness.

Consequently, James has concluded his teaching at 5:6. The three distinctive evidences of genuine Christian experience, the cardinal virtues, have been discovered (1:18,26,27) and expounded in turn (2:1 – 5:6). What then remains? It remains for him to say that the main lines of Christian faith and life which he has stated are abidingly and unchangingly true, and that perseverance in these things must ever mark the genuine Christian. The forward glance to the end of the present age (5:3) and the coming judgment (5:5) prompts him to remind believers of the coming of the Lord (5:7–9) and to call them to be found so doing.

The last section of his letter is a genuine conclusion. It summarizes all that has been said, and at the same time puts it in a positive, forward-looking context. At the beginning of his letter, James instructed us how to live in a life of trials and temptations (1:2), and his prescription was patience (1:3,4) and prayer (1:5). It is to these two things that he returns at the end: 'Be patient, therefore' (5:7), a theme which continues until verse 12. But the resource for a life of patience is a life of prayer: 'Let him pray' says verse 13 to the troubled person, and continuing to verse 18, in every verse either by noun or verb, prayer is mentioned. Patience to endure, prayer to strengthen.

There is also a further link between the conclusion and the body of the letter. James expounded three Christian characteristics in order: loving concern (chapter 2), the controlled tongue (chapter 3), and the unstained life (4:1 – 5:6). His conclusion takes up these three items but in the reverse order: patient continuance in well-doing until the coming of the Lord (5:7–12), the characteristic use of the Christian tongue in praise and prayer (5:13–18), and the mutual and watchful concern that ought to mark Christian relationships (5:19,20).

5:7–12 The patience of hope

7 Be patient, therefore, brethren, until the coming of the Lord. Behold, the farmer waits for the precious fruit of the earth, being patient over it until it receives the early and the late rain. 8You also be patient. Establish your hearts, for the coming of the Lord is at hand. 9Do not grumble, brethren, against one another, that you may not be judged; behold, the Judge is standing at the doors. 10As an example of suffering and patience, brethren, take the prophets who spoke in the name of the Lord. 11Behold, we call those happy who were steadfast. You have heard of the steadfastness of Job, and you have seen the purpose of the Lord, how the Lord is compassionate and merciful.

12But above all, my brethren, do not swear, either by heaven or by earth or with any other oath, but let your yes be yes and your no be no, that you may not fall under condemnation.

The structure of these verses is as follows. In verses 7,8, he speaks of patience; in verse 9 he gives one of his great emphatic warnings about sins of speech. Then (verses 10,11) he renews the call to patience; and, finally, in verse 12 he returns to the topic of a possible sin of speech.

a. The fruitfulness of patience (verses 7–9)

The two sub-sections of these verses, then, consist of a call to patience ending, in each case, with a warning against sins of speech. The first call to patience centres on an illustration taken from farming and has as its main thought the fruitfulness of Christian endurance. In our opening up of the verses we will follow through the farming metaphor.

First, James speaks of cultivating the fruit (verses 7,8). Behind the metaphor lies the teaching which was given at the beginning of the epistle, namely that as faith meets and passes the tests of life, it grows, by patience, into full maturity of character. So here there is obedience which, under testing, displays constancy, and is held on course by hope. In the farming world, patience is a fruitful virtue. The farmer sets out to obey the laws of God as they concern the world of nature, and then, having obeyed, he waits trustfully. But his patience is tested by the *early and the late rain*, not one buffeting but two. The *early*, or autumn, rain prepared the soil for the seed and the seed for germination. The *late*, or spring, rain swelled the grain in the ear to give a rich crop. There would be no germination and no development without the buffeting storms. But the end of the process is the *precious fruit of the earth*. It is a known and longed-for outcome, a sure hope which strengthens the farmer through the waiting days.

For us also (verse 8) the same principles apply: the obedience of faith, the testings of life, patient constancy, all held in place by a great hope. James faithfully warns us against the old enemy of inconsistency. He looks for the heart fixed upon God, the heart which leaves no room for the 'double mind'.[2] But with equal faithfulness he reminds us of our hope. James puts himself here in line with the main New Testament emphasis about the coming of Christ. It is so easy for us to be led off into very attractive paths of study, and even of speculation, and to forget the main reason why the New Testament so constantly calls us to think of our returning Lord. We can become side-tracked into a main consideration of the circumstances of His coming, or what state the world will be in, and will this or that have happened before or after.

All these are sometimes interesting and important questions, but James puts his finger on the main emphases concerning the returning Lord: first that His return is *at hand*. It has been so from the day of the apostles. James was not mistaken even though he lived over 1,000 years ago. The return of the Lord was then at hand; the return of the Lord is now at hand. We live in the last days, the days of the imminent return. And, secondly, the pressure upon us of that return is not to promote curiosity as to the date and circumstances, but to promote the life of holiness and of fruitfulness, so that we may be ready to meet the Lord.

We must also safeguard the crop that this patience is to bring forth (verse 9). In times of stress when we are receiving the 'early and the late rain' of God, impatience can easily show itself in the realm of the tongue. When the pressure of life is on, we may thoughtlessly wound our Christian brothers and sisters by hurtful remarks and so mar the fellowship in which alone the fruit will grow, for 'the harvest of righteousness is sown in peace by those who make peace' (3:18). If we detroy peace by our tongue, we mar the crop,

---

[2] R. A. Ward, *New Bible Commentary Revised*, interestingly compares the 'established (made firm, strong; well-founded) heart' of verse 8 with the 'fattened heart' of verse 5.

and enter the presence of that returning Lord, not with joy, but with fearful trembling before *the Judge* who *is standing at the doors*,[3] for to sin against our brethren with our tongue is to disobey the royal law itself (2:8).[4]

b. The blessedness of patience (verses 10–12)

James takes us from the fruitfulness of patience to the blessedness of patience. The first blessedness of patience is that God looks for patience in the life of His chosen servants (verse 10).[5] He visited the prophets with suffering and they manifested patience. It was not a sign of divine disapproval; it was a mark of God's approval upon them that He trusted them to suffer for His name's sake. Patience is a mark that God looks for in a chosen servant.

The second blessedness of patience is that God blesses His church through patient service (verse 11a). James here brings two thoughts into touch with each other: when we look back to the prophets we do so with great gratitude. We applaud them; we say, 'What wonderful men! How marvellous to have had such dealings with God and with men for God! What privileges they enjoyed!' But do we realize that we are congratulating sufferers? It is their meeting and passing triumphantly through their trials[6] that has made them objects of our praise. Apart from this we would not know them. Consequently they are to us not just an instance

[3] *Cf.* Jesus' own words, Mk. 13:29.
[4] *Grumble* (verse 9) is literally 'groan' or 'moan'. NEB is interpretatively exact: 'Do not blame your troubles on one another.' *Cf.* 'Speak evil', 4:11; note also Mt. 7:1–5.
[5] James stresses the prophets' fidelity to the message God gave them to deliver. In fact this is all he says about their life and work. *Cf.* Mitton, 'Faithfulness to God's commands so far from giving them immunity from suffering actually involved them in it.' Their privilege and their trials went hand in hand.
[6] *Cf.* Je. 11:21ff.; 20:1ff.; Ezk. 24:15ff.; Dn. 1:1–3,6; 6:16ff.; Ho. 1–3; Am. 7:10ff.; Heb. 11:32ff. *Cf.* Jerusalem Bible, 'Remember it is those who had endurance that we say are the blessed ones.'

of suffering but *an example* (verse 10), a headline copy for our imitation, and their example includes the encouragement that through His patient servants God enriches His church.

The third blessedness of patience is that God reveals Himself to His patient servants (verse 11b). The story of Job has come to us as an example of human steadfastness, but even more as a demonstration of divine purposefulness, and this is the point on which James would have us dwell. The word translated *purpose* indicates that the felicity which came at length to Job was not a fairy-tale way in which this particular man's experience happened to end but was rather the chosen divine objective from the beginning. Above all else it was the enrichment of knowing God more fully. Job ended with a greater testimony than he had ever had before: 'I had heard of thee by the hearing of the ear, but now my eye sees thee' (Jb. 42:5). James does not exclude the renewed earthly prosperity of Job (Jb. 42:10ff.) from his purview but he does emphasize what came to be freshly known about God, *how the Lord is compassionate and merciful*. To Job this knowledge was as vivid as the replacement of hearsay by personal encounter, but it did not come about in any other way than as the fruit of endurance through a long period of intense trial.[7]

Once more, however (verse 12), the blessing must be safeguarded. James warns here about anything other than straightforward, truthful speech. The blessing can be jeopardized if in a moment of impatience we fail to control our tongue and we rush to emphasize and underline the truthfulness of what we are saying by oaths, or when, in a moment of

---

[7]The word translated *compassionate* (Gk. *polusplanchnos*) is not found elsewhere (*cf.* the similar compound, *eusplanchnos*, in Eph. 4:32; 1 Pet. 3:8). Alford well suggests that it is a coinage designed to express 'abounding in steadfast love' (Heb. *rab hesed*, Ex. 34:6; LXX, *polueleos*). Coupled with the word *merciful*, which contains the thought of sharing the emotion of grief, the compound idea is that the Lord never relaxes His loving hold nor fails in loving sympathy.

impatience, we even rush to curses. He may be looking back to the prophets who *spoke in the name of the Lord* (verse 10). The word of truth was sufficient for those chosen men. They did not need to emphasize it by any merely human energy of oath-taking. But whether James had this example in mind or not, it does serve to underline the point he is making. For all ordinary purposes the Christian should covet to be known for straightforward, irreproachable truthfulness of speech. People should know by the proof of experience that he will stand to his 'yes' or 'no' without further ado.[8]

The importance of this to James cannot be over-stressed. It is to be watched *above all*, as a most certain way by which we would fall into the judgment of the returning Lord. The objective towards which our gracious Lord is aiming is surely no less than was His purpose with Job, to bring us at His return into an incomparably vivid experience of His steadfast love and mercy. But our mischievous sins of speech could mean that the glory comes clouded with judgment, and that the rapture with which we should greet Him will be diminished by a foreboding of His displeasure. In this context, James would have us 'above all' guard and discipline our tongues, lest we lose the reward of blessedness which God designed for patient servants.

[8]It is very unlikely that James would find any difficulty in the taking of an oath as required from witnesses in court, or that he intended any reference to such. Apart from the fact that it is absurd to expect strangers to be able to recognize at once that sterling quality of character which could not tell a lie, and therefore the request for a spoken guarantee of truth simply reflects our inevitable involvement in a society of sinners, the formal oath is, in the context of a court of law, part of the way in which we safeguard that control of speech on which James is so insistent. It is a solemn and considered use of the tongue which could come under no condemnation. Mt. 23:16–22 fills in the background of a society in which oath-taking was made part of a complicated scheme of evasion of responsibility and confidence trickery. The use of an oath with intent to deceive is far removed from the taking of an oath as a guarantee of truth. Solemn oath-taking is countenanced throughout Scripture: *e.g.* Dt. 4:26; 6:13; Je. 12:16; 2 Tim. 4:1.

13 Is any one among you suffering? Let him pray. Is any cheerful? Let him sing praise. **14**Is any among you sick? Let him call for the elders of the church, and let them pray over him, anointing him with oil in the name of the Lord; **15**and the prayer of faith will save the sick man, and the Lord will raise him up; and if he has committed sins, he will be forgiven. **16**Therefore confess your sins to one another, and pray for one another, that you may be healed. The prayer of a righteous man has great power in its effects. **17**Elijah was a man of like nature with ourselves and he prayed fervently that it might not rain, and for three years and six months it did not rain on the earth. **18**Then he prayed again and the heaven gave rain, and the earth brought forth its fruit.

Prayer is clearly the topic of these verses because it occurs, either as a noun or as a verb, in every one of them without exception. The connection with the preceding passage may be understood by saying that first of all, for the life of patience, he calls on us to lay hold on the strength of prayer as he did previously in 1:2–5. But secondly, he calls us to a characteristic Christian use of the tongue; and in many ways the antidote to loose or impatient speech would be to speak often and much with the Lord. Here is the proper use for the Christian tongue, and here are divine resources to enable us to live the life of patience, to reap the fruit, and to inherit the blessing.

There are four people at prayer in verses 13–18:

a. The individual at prayer (verse 13)

This is a wonderfully full verse, and one which asserts fundamental principles which James is about to apply in a most important area of Christian thought and experience. Its main points can be stated under three headings. Firstly, the Christian has a religion for all life. In their way the words 'trouble' and 'joy' cover the whole of life's experiences, and each of them can be the cause, and often is the cause of spiritual upset. Suffering and trouble easily give rise to an attitude of surly rebellion against God, leading to the abandonment of all spiritual practices. Equally often, times of ease and affluence beget complacency, laziness and the assumption that we are able of ourselves to cope with life, and God is forgotten. James is clearly aware of this, for the persistence, throughout his letter, of the themes of trial and suffering, as well as the warnings against allowing the heart to stray from God after uncertain riches, indicate his acquaintance with the full run of life and his concern to armour us against its varied assaults. But his insistence is that none of these things should move us. Neither suffering nor ease should find us without a suitable Christian response in prayer and song.[1]

Secondly, the Christian has a God for every circumstance. In suffering and trouble, prayer, and in times of joyful ease, praise both acknowledge the sufficiency of God. To pray to Him is to acknowledge His sovereign power to meet our need, and to praise is to acknowledge His sovereign power in appointing our circumstances. Thus, whether viewed as the source of supply in need, or the source of benefit in joy, God is our sufficiency. This leads at once to the third observation: the Christian has a resource for personal use, namely, that in every circumstance of life we flee to God. Are we in trouble? We flee to Him. Are we in joy? We flee to Him. The Christian life is an exercise in practised consecration, to 'hallow every pleasure, sanctify each pain'. Our whole life,

---

[1] *Suffering* (verse 13) is wider than the sufferings of sickness. *Cf.* 2 Tim. 2:9; 4:5. The cognate noun 'suffering' was used in verse 10 for the varied trials of the prophets. We may rightly say, therefore, that James is asserting principles in verse 13 which cover all aspects of life under the most widely conceived categories. Calvin rightly catches this in his comment that 'he means that there is no time in which God does not invite us to himself'. Tasker perceptively notes that 'when Jesus was in *agony*, wrestling with the forces of evil at the moment of their strongest attack, . . . "he prayed more earnestly" (Lk. xxii.44)', and adds the comment, 'Prayer may not remove the affliction but it most certainly can transform it.'

as we might say, should be so angled towards God that whatever strikes upon us, whether sorrow or joy, should be deflected upwards at once into His presence.

But in particular this exercise in practised consecration is an exercise in glad acceptance of the will of God. This is the common denominator of prayer and praise. In praise, we say to God, Your will is good, perfect, and acceptable; this is what You have done for me, and I rejoice. And as for prayer in time of trouble, it attempts – however poorly we may succeed – to copy the Gethsemane prayer of the Lord Jesus, 'Not my will, but thine, be done' (Lk. 22:42).

This is the individual at prayer. He is reflecting all his life upward in acknowledging the sufficiency and the sovereignty of his God, and practising the grace of acceptance, not the disgrace of stubbornness. He is not saying, 'God, You have done this to me, but I am going to pester You until You do something else.' He is saying to His heavenly Father, in prayer and in praise: 'The will of God is good and perfect and acceptable; Thy will be done.'

b. The elders at prayer (verses 14,15)

Now we come to a most fascinating section in the writing of James, for we have the elders engaging in prayer at the behest of a sick person.

Two questions will help to open up these verses for us. We will ask first, How are we to approach this passage? For many different lines of approach have been tried, and it is necessary to clear the ground of false ideas and interpretations. Secondly, we will move on to the positive question, What, then, does the passage teach?

First, then, how are we to approach these verses? There are some who have said that we have here a ministry of healing which was either exercised only by the apostles or else was confined to apostolic times, but which has now ceased to be available to the church. This view, however, does not coincide with James' invitation to the sick person to call *the elders*. By using this title, he associates this ministry to the sick, not with the unique and irreplaceable apostolate, nor with the long-passed apostolic age, but with the continuing leadership in the local church, a leadership which, though in differing forms and under differing titles, has ever been and still is present and available. We cannot, therefore, agree that James here describes a bygone ministry.

Another approach is that of the Roman Catholic Church which has made use of this passage in order to provide a sort of long-distance justification for the practice of Extreme Unction, a ministry of anointing applied to people who are in imminent expectation of death, in order to prepare them for death and for the world to come.[2] Again, however, we are bound to say that this is not what James is describing. For example, he does not say what sort of illness is involved here, whether serious or comparatively trivial. His words are completely general. In any sickness whatever, the person concerned is at liberty to send for the elders of the church. Neither does James say anything about imminent death; in fact, quite the reverse. The person, far from being expected to die, in these verses is, if anything, rather expected to recover.

Then again, there are others who say that, in the providence of God, medical science has been given to us. God has increased our knowledge both in medicine and in surgery, and He has designed, therefore, that what was a purely ecclesiastical transaction in the church should now pass into

[2]*Cf.* the marginal comment on verse 14 in the Jerusalem Bible: 'The tradition that these prayers and this anointing with oil in the name of the Lord, and for the purpose of helping the sick and forgiving their sins, are the origin of the Church's "sacrament of the sick" (or Holy Unction), was endorsed by the Council of Trent.' The teaching can be studied in full in the three chapters under the heading 'On the Sacrament of Extreme Unction', Session XIV of the Council of Trent.

the hands of the medical services. This passage, they would say, belongs to those situations in which no medical help was available. Now there is some truth in this. In the New Testament itself there is a clear indication of the use of such medical science as was available. For example, the good Samaritan poured on oil and wine (Lk. 10:34), that is to say, he resorted to the customary medicines of the day, the oil to soothe and the wine to cleanse. Paul, writing to Timothy, urged him to use no longer water but a little wine 'for the sake of your stomach and your frequent ailments' (1 Tim. 5:23). He did not urge Timothy to send for the elders of the church. He advised a medical solution of his problem. Likewise, Paul also reports on one occasion that he had left Trophimus ill at Miletus (2 Tim. 4:20). This piece of evidence has the negative value of showing that Paul did not conceive it to be his apostolic duty to apply powers of miraculous spiritual healing to every case of sickness, nor did Trophimus feel it right to call for such a ministry. Paul furthermore speaks of Luke as 'the beloved physician' (Col. 4:14), and this must at the very least mean that he approved of Luke's medical skill both in its existence and in its exercise. It may, of course, very well imply that Paul himself had reason to be grateful to the medical ability of his companion.

Thus the New Testament recognizes a medical approach to sickness, alongside what may be called the spiritual or miraculous approach. It would seem most likely that James is here stating an approach to sickness which in given circumstances can be parallel to or even replace the application of medicines.

The three different views outlined above have begun to open up the meaning of the verses for us. It is now possible, though it will necessarily involve some repetition, to turn to the second question, What do these verses teach?

Firstly, they teach that there is a continuing ministry to the sick in the local church, vested in 'the elders'. It is not a ministry exclusive to a particular person, such as an apostle, or someone who claims to have from God the gift of healing. The leaders of the local church have been given the ministry which James describes, and it must be held to continue to this day.

Secondly, the sick person must desire this ministry. James says, *Let him call for the elders* (verse 14). This is a permission, not a direction. He may call; he is not obliged to do so. Paul's leaving of Trophimus ill, and his recommendation to Timothy of medical remedies imply, as we have seen, that there is not necessarily in every case the demand for this ministration, and that it is not always right to apply it. But the ministry of the elders is there for the sick person who seeks it.

Thirdly, there is a dimension of healing besides that of healing the body. *If he has committed sins, he will be forgiven* (verse 15).

There are three possibilities here. One is that, lying on his sick-bed, he becomes aware that his sickness is due to sin. Or secondly, lying on his sick-bed, by self-examination he becomes aware of sins that he had forgotten: they did not cause his illness, but his illness was the opportunity of remembering them. Or, thirdly, lying ill, he recognizes that he cannot be ever completely whole unless he is also completely reconciled to God. Therefore he sends for the leaders of his church for a ministry of prayer and of anointing in the name of the Lord.

Fourthly, we come to the centrally important truth of the passage: this ministry of healing is subject to the laws of prayer. When the elders come at the invitation of the sick, they anoint him *with oil in the name of the Lord* (verse 14). By the anointing they give him symbolic assurance that the Holy Spirit, the Lord and Giver of life, is active and involved in his situation. By using the name of the Lord they indicate that only Christ can, in fact, heal him. But so far as a human agency of healing is concerned, they are to pray over him, and (verse 15) *The prayer of faith will save the sick man*. This ministry to the sick is not, in the first instance, a ministry of anointing but a ministry of praying. It is the prayer of faith that will save the sick. But does not that involve us in saying, as a principle, that the ministry of healing is subject to the laws that govern prayer? By this means we have a correct and biblical way of understanding the very positive promise that *the prayer of faith will save the sick man, and the Lord will raise him up*.[3]

This is the standard and customary way in which the Bible makes its promises concerning prayer. For example, 'If two of you agree on earth about anything they ask, it will be done for them by my Father in heaven' (Mt. 18:19); or again, 'Whatever you ask in prayer, you will receive, if you have faith' (Mt. 21:22); or again, 'Whatever you ask in my name, I will do it' (Jn. 14:13). Alongside them, place also this prayer-promise: *The prayer of faith will save the sick man*.

How do we understand these unqualified assurances concerning answers to prayer? We know from the Word of God and from confirmatory evidence in our own lives that these promises are expressed as great affirmations, first to assure us of the generosity of God who will withhold from us nothing that is good and, secondly, to assure us of the liberty of asking given to us, whereby there is nothing we cannot ask of God. But the one thing these promises do not imply is that God allows us to be stubborn in His presence and insistent on what we think is right. Indeed if it were the case that whatever we ask, God was pledged to give, then we would soon cease to pray, because we would not have sufficient confi-

[3]*Cf*. A. Barnes, *Notes on the New Testament* (London, 1840): 'This must be understood, as such promises are everywhere, with this restriction, that they shall be restored to health if it shall be the will of God. . . . It cannot be taken in the absolute and unconditional sense, for then . . . the sick person would always recover, no matter how often he might be sick, and he need never die.'

dence in our own wisdom to ask God for anything. It would impose an intolerable burden on frail human wisdom if by His prayer-promises God was pledged to give whatever we ask, when we ask it, and in exactly the terms we ask. How could we bear the burden?

But, as we saw (verse 13), the essence of prayer is 'Thy will be done'. When a man comes to God to pray in time of trouble, to praise in time of joy, he is in effect blessing God because His will is a sovereign will. In other words, in the prayer of faith, our faith is not that the promises will be fulfilled just like that; it is the faith which rests trustfully on the will of a sovereign, gracious and loving God. What this sick person desires in his sickness is the emphatic assurance of the goodness of God around him, of the fellowship of prayer around him. He intends not to insist on his own will, for that is the way of insecurity, but to put himself within the complete, eternal security of the unchangeable and the unchangeably gracious will of God.

We may with profit pause briefly to consider the will of God in relation to our prayers. Must we always say, 'Thy will be done'? The Bible would answer with an unqualified affirmative. This is the way Jesus has taught us to pray (Mt. 6:10) in the prayer on which all prayers are to be modelled; this is the way Jesus prayed (Mt. 26:39–44) and He is our model in all things. What is the effect of making this petition in relation to all our petitions? Its effect is to take away from our prayers all the limitations of our knowledge of what our real needs are, all the limitations of our proposals for the meeting of our needs, and to place ourselves and our needs unreservedly into the hands of that infinite wisdom, love and power which is our heavenly Father's. To say 'Thy will be done' does not impose a restriction on what we ask; it lifts the restrictions. And it is relevant to say that this is more important in the case of a sick person than in almost any other case: the disposing of the welfare of a child of God cannot be left with greater confidence anywhere else than in the Father's hands, nor can any solution of the plight be more fitting, beneficial and glorious than that which He has in mind.

c. The friends at prayer (verse 16a)

The word *therefore* (omitted by AV) is important. We may explain its meaning in this way: seeing that prayer is such a wonderful thing, seeing that we can bring our sick friends to God in prayer, and the sick ones can invite the elders to come and pray, and God has pledged Himself along these lines in the generosity of prayer, then surely we should be enthusiastic to lay hold on the agency of prayer in all manner of life's situations. James is helping us to take these principles of prayer and apply them in a new situation which contrasts with the former. There (verses 14,15) the matter was sickness, now (verse 16) the matter is sin, and James here uses the word 'to heal' as it is often used in the Bible, of the healing of the sickness of sin.[4] Now, when the situation is one of sin and the desire to be rid of it, what are we to do? We are to involve ourselves in the fellowship of prayer. The temptations of life are upon us. We are threatened by sin, and we go to a fellow-Christian with the request, 'Will you come and pray with me? I have a burden to share.'

Now this is a very serious thing to do, for it involves laying the heart bare before someone else. Indeed, it is a very serious thing also to be the recipient of such a confidence. Yet it is clearly something we should be doing as Christians. We should be involving each other in bonds of confidence and prayer. But before we do so we ought to be very careful indeed to observe the two rules which James makes for this sort of mutual care. When he says . . . *and pray one for another* he is declaring that there should be no hearing of someone else's admissions of sin and need without a deliberate and single-

[4]*E.g.* Pss. 103:3; 107:17–20; Is. 6:10; 53:4 (note RSV mg.); 1 Pet. 2:24.

minded intention to make it a matter of prayer. Only thus will we be delivered from the spirit of prying curiosity which, far from helping the needy out of his sin, would make the whole thing a matter of sin to the listener.

James' second rule is that there must be no confession without the determination to be healed, to be rid of that sin. Notice how clearly that is stated to be the aim of the fellowship: . . . *that you may be healed.* Just as the listener needs to examine his motives, to purge himself of all idle curiosity, and to bring himself to the sole intention of praying for his friend, so the speaker must also examine his motives, for the sin could often be confessed in a spirit of exhibitionism, and without any real abhorrence of it or longing to see it gone. But, where the motives are right, what a gracious thing James urges upon us in this mutual ministry of praying friends!

d. The prophet at prayer (verses 16b–18)

Even though it is helpful to divide the passage up like this, we ought to notice that James allows the subject of prayer to develop naturally. The place of prayer in all life (verse 13) led him to show the place of prayer in sickness (verses 14, 15), and then to bring the same power to bear on another area of our problems, that of sin and its cure (verse 16a). Now he continues, still concerned to share with us the privilege and potency of prayer, by stating a truth and illustrating it in the life of Elijah.

The truth is that *the prayer of a righteous man has great power in its effects* (verse 16b). Note three points. First, the inherent power of prayer. It *has great power.* The word used points to native or inherent strength. Perhaps we might speak of 'untapped resources'. The most unpromising tracts of land conceal beneath them rich oil wells, seams of gold; grey seas cover deposits of natural gas. This is the picture suggested by the word used – not the unpromising face of the landscape but the immensity of the concealed power. In human terms, when we speak of the situation producing the man, we mean that in a given set of circumstances hitherto unthought-of powers of wisdom, leadership, strength of character and purpose come to light. So it is with prayer. It has great resources waiting to be tapped; immense potency there to be put to use.

Secondly, the effective application of prayer. *In its effects* translates a word which the New Testament uses to describe work which achieves its aim. For example, it is used of the Lord Jesus, referring to 'the power which enables him even to subject all things to himself' (Phil. 3:21). This effectual energy is here attributed to prayer. When we pray about a matter we bring all the inherent power of prayer to bear upon a particular point and it becomes effective in its accomplishment there.

Thirdly, there is the spiritual foundation of prayer. It is the prayer of *a righteous man.* If prayer is to bring its inherent power into play effectively, it must proceed from a life that is right with God. It is at this point that James introduces the illustration of Elijah, and he does so for our reassurance. The word *righteous* has a forbidding ring. Understood in the sense of complete moral integrity, it would exclude us from all possibility of ever exercising effective prayer. But is this what James means? Elijah, we are told, was a man *of like nature with ourselves* (verse 17). He was not sinlessly perfect, but what was true of him can equally be true of us: he was right with God. Those who by grace have been given a footing of righteousness in God's sight have thus been introduced into the spiritual realm where effective prayer belongs, and it is of right for them to make use of it.

James has now cleared the ground, and with the help of the illustration of Elijah he can tell us a fourth – and the greatest – truth about prayer: the supernatural results of prayer. 'Of like nature with ourselves' becomes in NEB 'with human frailties like our own' and this catches the spirit of James' words exactly. Elijah was an ordinary human being. But when he prayed there was a supernatural result, *it did not rain. . . . Then he prayed again and the heaven gave rain, and the earth brought forth its fruit* (verses 17, 18). But these are things which God alone can do. To give or withhold rain, to give or withhold fruitfulness are divine activities. Prayer, then, brings two things together, a human agent and a supernatural result. By means of prayer a mere human can move God.

In Elijah's case this happened when he *prayed fervently* (verse 17). To our ears that suggests intensity of prayer, but the meaning rather ought to be this, that he 'gave himself to prayer'. It was not his intensity that mattered, but that he resorted to prayer alone. He did nothing about it but pray, and that prayer moved God.

5:19, 20 The fellowship of concern

19 My brethren, if any one among you wanders from the truth and some one brings him back, ²⁰let him know that whoever brings back a sinner from the error of his way will save his soul from death and will cover a multitude of sins.

So James brings us through this wonderful little passage dealing with the characteristic use of the Christian tongue, the Christian flying in prayer to the resources which will enable him to live the life of patience.

In the last two verses of the epistle he raises again the third of the great central truths of Christian living: the fellowship of concern (5:19,20, corresponding to 2:1–26).

There are two sides to Christian helpfulness. Verse 16 showed us one side: a needy Christian turning for help to another Christian. But the other side is this: a Christian sees another Christian in need and runs to help him, without waiting to be asked. He runs after him out of care for his soul. The Christian church is a fellowship of mutual concern.

a. The agents involved

My brethren, if any one among you wanders from the truth, and some one brings him back . . . In the Christian fellowship somebody is beginning to backslide. The responsibility for recovering him rests with *some one*. James does not say 'your minister', nor 'one of your elders', nor 'your ruling elder', nor 'a church officer', nor even 'a mature Christian'. He says 'someone'. The agent in the recovery of the backslider is the other church member who sees his fellow-believer in spiritual need. This is a relationship of mutual concern without qualification. The word translated *some one* is completely indefinite. To see a fellow-Christian moving away from the Lord is to be responsible to run to his aid.

b. The issues involved

James now sharpens our awareness of our responsibility towards each other's spiritual welfare by clarifying the issues involved. They are issues which involve the mind, the life, and the destiny.

As to the mind, it is losing its grip on God's truth: *If any one among you wanders from the truth* (verse 19). The truth is the means of our salvation (1:18; *cf*. Eph. 1:13) and the means of our growth (1:21; *cf*. 1 Pet. 2:2). To lose one's grip on the truth is to lose touch with spiritual vitality. In consequence, the next thing to suffer is the life, which loses its grip upon holiness: to *wander from the truth* becomes *the error of his way* (verse 20). What happens in the mind is quickly reflected in the outward walk. Just as the mind is the key to sanctification, so that we are 'transformed by the renewal of your mind' (Rom. 12:2), so the mind is the key factor in backsliding (Eph. 4:17,18). When the mind loses touch with divine truth the life loses the savour of God-pleasing holiness.

But there is a matter of destiny involved also: *whoever brings back a sinner . . . will save his soul from death* (verse 20). What can this mean? Let us first be certain of one thing. It is a clear truth of Scripture that we cannot be saved today and lost tomorrow. The Lord Jesus gives us an eternal security (Jn. 10:28; Eph. 2:4–10). Our conversion is a genuine passing from death to life, leaving the darkness of Satan's empire for the light of God's kingdom (Col. 1:12–14), and we are those whom God has already 'qualified . . . to share in the inheritance of the saints in light'. If this is the case, how can the backslider need to be saved all over again from spiritual death?

We need to ask another question before we can find the answer to this one. To whom is our eternal security known? It is known first of all to God. We read that 'the Lord knows those who are his' (2 Tim. 2:19). Secondly, it is made known to us ourselves as a matter of Christian assurance by 'the Spirit himself bearing witness with our spirit that we are children of God, and if children, then heirs, heirs of God, and fellow heirs with Christ . . .' (Rom. 8:16,17). But as far as other people are concerned, our eternal security is at best an inference they make from what they hear us say and see us do. They are bound to judge us by this test: 'Let every one who names the name of the Lord depart from iniquity' (2 Tim. 2:19). Now, the present verses in James are not written from the point of view of what God knows about us, nor from the point of view of what we know about ourselves, but from the point of view of our fellow-Christians, observing our lives and hearing our talk. To them the evidence of backsliding in our lives must call in question whether we are truly Christ's or not, for at that moment they see us failing to pass the only test which they can apply, namely that we profess to name the name of the Lord but we are not departing from unrighteousness.

It is in this connection that James urges that destiny is involved when Christians slip away from the Lord. We must look on each other as those who profess Christ, and our great concern must be to shepherd each other right through to eternity. We must learn to see each evidence of backsliding as if it were evidence that that person had never really taken saving hold of Christ at all. We must run to them. We must recover them for Him.

c. The effort involved

In a final observation on James' teaching, let us take note of the verbs he uses here to describe what we must do for each other as we undertake the task of mutual shepherding and loving care: *brings back . . . save . . . cover a multitude of sins*. We know full well that these express things which only God, in Christ, by the Holy Spirit can do. They express the various aspects of the work of salvation. God alone can bring the sinner back (Jn. 6:44), rescue him from eternal death (Col. 1:12,13), and wipe away his sins (Eph. 1:7). How then can we perform these great tasks in relation to each other?

The answer is that we cannot, but we must act as if we could. The verbs express the measure of the effort to which God calls us in expressing our spiritual concern for each other. Though we cannot convert them, we must labour to do so; though we cannot rescue them from death, we must strive for their souls as if their destiny rested with us; though we cannot cover their sins we must follow the example of the Son of God who can do so, and hold nothing dear to ourselves and no sacrifice too great if only they are saved.[5]

James has nothing more to say: no benediction, no doxology, no grace. We must not try to end our studies any less

[5] *Cf.* Jn. 20:23; Rom. 11:14; 1 Cor. 7:16; 9:22; 1 Tim. 4:16.

abruptly than he has ended his letter. He does not wish any word or gesture of farewell to deflect our minds from this astonishing, terrifying, yet wonderful truth, that the fellowship we have as Christians is a fellowship of loving concern in which each of us is to act towards the other as God in Christ has acted towards us.